He'll forgive
me anyway

HE'LL FORGIVE
me anyway

The Deadly Lie of
Marshmallow Grace

STEVE HALLIDAY

GENERAL EDITOR: STEVE KEELS

BROADMAN
&HOLMAN
PUBLISHERS

NASHVILLE, TENNESSEE

13-digit ISBN: 978-0-8054-2752-3
10-digit ISBN: 0-8054-2752-X

Published by Broadman & Holman Publishers,
Nashville, Tennessee

Dewey Decimal Classification: 234.1
Subject Heading: GRACE (THEOLOGY) \ SIN \ CHRISTIAN LIFE

For emphasis,
the author made many words and phrases in Scriptures italics.

1 2 3 4 5 6 7 8 9 10 09 08 07 06 05

For my niece and nephew, Nichole and Ryan:

May the grace of God sweep you up into
the best life Jesus has to offer.

Contents

For it is by grace you have been saved, through faith—
and this not from yourselves, it is the gift of God—
not by works, so that no one can boast.
For we are God's workmanship,
created in Christ Jesus to do good works,
which God prepared in advance for us to do.

EPHESIANS 2:8–10

INTRODUCTION

-vvvv-

When Something Really Good Goes Really Bad

*I*n my bachelor years I saw it happen all the time. I'd put a delicious piece of pizza or a flavorful container of Chinese food in the refrigerator and then forget about them. I didn't mean to, but new items inevitably pushed old ones to the back of the shelf. And three months later, I discovered that my tasty treats had turned into fuzzy, green globs of . . . something.

Now, I really like Chinese food. I take great pleasure in Italian cuisine. But I found that if I mistreated them or used them in a way the cooks never intended, they became something . . . else.

I believe a similar thing may happen with one of God's all-time greatest gifts to us: His grace. Through His grace, we can escape hell and enjoy heaven. Through His grace, we can defeat Satan and spend thrilling times with Christ. Through His grace, we can avoid despair and grab ultimate satisfaction. Through His grace, we can build deep and fulfilling relationships with others, find creative ways to serve our community and our world, and, perhaps most exciting of all, introduce friends and others to Jesus Christ and the amazing grace that He offers them too.

Grace is *great!*

But what happens when we push it into a corner of the refrigerator that God never intended? What becomes of it when we treat it in a way the Cook has forbidden?

Because I don't like the image forming in my head, let's change the image. Forget about refrigerators and cooks for a moment, but don't forget about food. Food is good, so let's stick with that.

Suppose a friend asked you to celebrate a traditional Thanksgiving dinner with her family. That's how she advertised it: a traditional Thanksgiving dinner, complete with all the trimmings. You eagerly agree, and you spend several days dreaming of moist turkey, garlic mashed potatoes, homemade pumpkin pie, and all the rest. You can hardly wait.

The big day finally comes, and you arrive at your friend's house full of anticipation. You sit anxiously in the living room while the food gets carried to the dining room. At last you take a big whiff— and your eyes fly open with alarm. Something smells amiss.

In a few minutes your host ushers you to your seat . . . and you can hardly believe your eyes. You see not a turkey but a slab of tofu. No mashed potatoes but a pile of soybean pilaf. No pumpkin pie but something that looks suspiciously like a failed marriage between Egg Beaters and Spam. And instantly you know the truth: *I've been slimed!*

Now, would you fault the real turkey for its tofu counterfeit? Would you blame genuine mashed potatoes for the existence of a soybean phony? Would you condemn an authentic pumpkin pie for the appearance of a hybrid fraud? Hardly. But you'd still be chomping at the bit for the real thing.

I think a lot of folks these days are chomping at the bit for genuine *grace*—even though many of them don't even know they've been eating at a table full of counterfeits. They've been nibbling on marshmallow grace for a long time, and it *does* taste sweet; yet they can't quite figure out why they feel hungry all the time. If they look in the mirror they might see their teeth falling out, but they figure that's just part of the deal because they see so many other people whose teeth are also falling out.

How much healthier and happier they'd be if they recognized the counterfeit in their mouths and, instead, started feasting on the genuine article! Authentic grace might be a little harder to chew than marshmallows, but it does a whole lot better job of building up the body. And over time, it can even repair and replace rotten teeth.

This book represents my attempt at exposing the dangers of the counterfeit (marshmallow grace) and, instead, encouraging believers in Christ to partake of the genuine article (real grace). Real grace, of course, is not jawbreaker grace, another counterfeit that errs in the opposite direction (see chap. 8, "The Real Deal"). But that's for later.

For now, I invite you to dig in and chow down on what God might want to say to you through the following pages. If I've wandered too far one way or another, I apologize ahead of time; I'll pray that God would not only show both of us the truth, but that He'd give us a love for it (and for Him and for His people) as well.

One last thing, and I hope you won't hold it against me. Although this is a book intended mostly for teens, I'm not a youth pastor, a teen speaker, or anything like that. Whenever I do get the chance to talk to high school students, I always ask the same thing. I'd like to ask it of you, too. Would it be OK with you if I treat you not as a kid but as a young adult? I promise I'll make what follows as clear and helpful and entertaining as I can manage, but if you've opened this book looking for a wild and crazy time, I'm afraid you'll be disappointed. I don't know how to do the wild and crazy thing, and even if I did, I'm not sure I would. I like to have fun, of course. I like to laugh. I like to have a good time. And I hope in the next little bit we'll do all of that together, at least a good part of the time.

Mostly, however, this book is for those who want to get serious about their relationship with Jesus. It's for those who want to think deeply about what the Bible says about grace and how God designed it to help us become mature and productive Christians. It's for those who, like me, want more than anything to honor God, enjoy Him and His world, and make a difference while we're here.

If that describes you, I think we'll have a great time together. And no tofu allowed.

PART 1

What's That Smell?

1

Pagan Believers

O ne hot, sunny afternoon in northern California, I lay dreamily atop an air mattress floating on a small lagoon in Lake Shasta. Once in awhile I slowly paddled myself away from energetic students engaged in water fights or from more subdued ones sunbathing.

And then I saw him, headed straight for me. His noisy splashing and intense manner announced that my break had come to an end.

"Are you the speaker guy?" he demanded.

"Yeah, I guess I am," I replied. That week I was not Steve Halliday, book editor, or Steve Halliday, writer, but Steve Halliday, speaker at our church's annual high school Houseboat Camp. A couple of hundred students and dozens of staff had descended on Lake Shasta for a hot week of water skiing, inner tubing, swimming, eating, morning Bible studies and nightly large group sessions (where I came in). I had been asked to address the topic of "courage."

"Yah. I thought so," he sputtered. He grabbed a flotation noodle and swam up right next to me. "Can I ask you a question?"

"Sure," I answered. "I'll tell you what I can."

He scrunched up his dripping nose and said, "Yeah, I was just wondering. Is it OK for a Christian to swear? I mean, when I get mad, I say things that we hear a lot in the R-rated movies. Is that OK?"

For the next few minutes we had a watery discussion about what it means to be a Christian. We talked a lot about grace and how God loved us so much that He sent His Son to die on the cross for us to pay the penalty for our sin. I explained how Jesus rose from the dead, proving His ability to save us. And I also tried to make clear that those who put their faith in Jesus are saved to live a new kind of life, totally unlike how they lived before and completely different from those without any faith in Christ.

"Language isn't really the issue," I said. "Faith in Christ is the issue. But once you put your faith in Jesus, why would you *want* to do the things that disappoint and anger Him? So far as your question about language is concerned, I'm pretty sure Jesus didn't have a potty mouth. And people who accept the salvation that Jesus offers want more than anything else to become like Him. That includes how they talk and how they behave."

We talked a little more, and in a few minutes he thanked me and swam away; but I didn't know for sure whether I had answered his question in a way that made sense to him. For a long time afterward I thought about how I might have explained more clearly what the Bible teaches about grace and how it's supposed to impact our lives after we become Christians.

This book is the result.

A Long-Time Problem

When I first started thinking about how to begin this chapter, I mentally debated whether I ought to tell a whole bunch of graphic stories about how a growing number of professing Christians treat salvation like eternal fire insurance—a ticket out of hell but nothing more. These believers *plan* to sin and ask forgiveness later. They be-have exactly like their non-Christian friends, whether the activities in question have to do with sex, alcohol, drugs, cheating, stealing, lying—whatever.

But I soon thought better of my plan. I doubt whether you need to hear any such lurid stories. In fact, you probably know a whole lot more of them than I do. Maybe you're even living them. If so, this book's for you.

I think a lot of Christians today have heard so much about the unconditional love of God and His amazing grace that they honestly don't think their behavior *matters*. And so they live like it.

Survey after survey in the past few years has revealed that the conduct of Christians doesn't differ much (if at all) from those who make no claim of faith in Christ. They cheat, steal, lie, sleep around, get drunk, get high, and generally go wild at just about the same rates as non-Christians. If a space alien were to silently watch them from orbit, he would detect zero difference between their behavior and that of anyone else.

I don't know whether such a discovery would upset the space alien, but I know it upsets God. I know it disappoints Jesus. The Lord not only expects that we will behave differently from pagans; He insists on it.

In His famous "Sermon on the Mount," Jesus raised the bar for what He expects of His disciples. Toward the end of His talk, He tells His followers that He

> *But Christian is as pagan does? That just doesn't work for Jesus.*

wants them to actually *love* their enemies—something unheard of. It's easy to love those who love you, Jesus says; non-Christians do that easily enough. Jesus, however, expects more from His followers: "What are you doing more than others? Do not even pagans do that? Be perfect, therefore, as your heavenly Father is perfect" (Matthew 5:47–48).

Jesus not only wants us to act in ways clearly distinct from pagans; He says He wants us to be "perfect . . . as your heavenly Father is perfect." Now, hold on! Just a moment! *Perfect* as God Himself is perfect? That's a pretty high bar! Yes, it is—but unless Jesus was just blowing smoke (something I doubt), He meant it.

Of course, we can become "perfect" only through faith in Christ, when God assigns to our account the perfection of Jesus. Yet it seems as though Jesus means more than this. At the very least, He requires His followers to behave in a radically different way than the non-Christians around them. If pagan is as pagan does, then it's equally true that Christian is as Christian does.

But Christian is as pagan does? That just doesn't work for Jesus.

Neither did it work for His disciples after Pentecost. Once the Holy Spirit began dwelling inside of them, enabling them to do what Jesus had called them to do, they started saying things like this:

> Live such good lives among the pagans that, though they
> accuse you of doing wrong, they may see your good deeds
> and glorify God on the day he visits us. (1 Peter 2:12)

You have spent enough time in the past doing what pagans choose to do—living in debauchery, lust, drunkenness, orgies, carousing and detestable idolatry. Of course, your former friends are very surprised when you no longer join them in the wicked things they do, and they say evil things about you. But just remember that they will have to face God, who will judge everyone, both the living and the dead. (1 Peter 4:3 NIV; vv. 4–5 NLT)

It greatly saddened and hurt the apostles whenever they discovered that some of the people they had led to faith in Christ had gone back to living like pagans. It made no sense to them. And so they sharply warned their friends to clean up their acts. Paul once wrote to the church at Corinth, "It is actually reported that there is sexual immorality among you, and of a kind that does not occur even among pagans: A man has his father's wife. And you are proud! Shouldn't you rather have been filled with grief and have put out of your fellowship the man who did this?" (1 Corinthians 5:1–2).

Paul couldn't understand how genuine believers could not only tolerate paganlike behavior in their church but actually accept it. Somehow, it didn't seem to trouble the Corinthians that a young man from their church was openly sleeping with his stepmother. They not only allowed the gross behavior to continue; apparently they accepted it. And *why* did they accept it? It seems likely that they fell victim to the same epidemic that plagues so many contemporary believers. They thought that the love and grace of God gave them permission to sin however they wanted, without fear of consequences. Many still think the same thing today.

They're wrong. And they put themselves in grave danger because of it.

Abused Grace

While the kind of thinking that encourages a believer in Christ to get "sin happy" has reached epidemic proportions, the problem is far from new. The apostle Paul had to deal with it even in the first churches ever planted.

By the time Paul wrote to the Christians in Rome (probably about AD 57), already the virus had begun to spread. He had never met the

Romans in person, yet he felt it necessary to warn them about a serious error making the rounds, an error that his enemies had tried to pin on him. Paul had been traveling around the Roman world, telling everyone about the wonderful grace of God that could take away their sins and give them a home in heaven. Yet some people misunderstood this message of grace and misrepresented it badly. They "slanderously reported" Paul as saying, "Let us do evil that good may result." The lie so infuriated Paul that he angrily wrote, "Their condemnation is deserved" (Romans 3:8).

Paul didn't want anyone to think of grace as a license to act out. Grace gave a believer the power to live for God, not the security to sin in safety. The problem had become so serious that the apostle brought it up twice more in the same letter.

In Romans 6:1–2, the apostle asks, "What shall we say, then? Shall we go on sinning so that grace may increase? By no means! We died to sin; how can we live in it any longer?" Paul had just described how the death of Christ gave Jesus the power to forgive the sins of every person who came to Him in faith. No matter how big or numerous the sins, the grace of Jesus could cover them all. Paul worried that some people who heard this Good News would think: *Great! The more I sin, the more grace I get! I think I'll go for it!*

People who think along these confused lines make comments like the one by an American cartoonist and writer, Jules Feiffer. "Christ died for our sins," he once said. "Dare we make his martyrdom meaningless by not committing them?"[1] A clever comment—but not a wise one. Believers who try to live like this set themselves up for a shipload of pain and regret.

Some other believers make a slightly more sophisticated error. They don't think, *sin more, get more grace*. They tell themselves, "I'm under grace, not under law. Therefore I can sin to my heart's content."

Paul countered such a sick view like this: "What then? Shall we sin because we are not under law but under grace? By no means!" (Romans 6:15). Paul taught the Romans that they became a slave to whoever or whatever they obeyed. If they obeyed their natural impulse to sin, then they became a slave to that sin. Remember, slaves don't get to choose what they do; they take orders from their master.

And what's the problem with making sin your master? Simple. Sin has only one reward for its slaves: death. So if you really want to die, Paul said, then go ahead and let sin rule (and ruin) your life.

Yet Paul had a deep concern even beyond such a grisly future. He knew that Christians who live like pagans hurt more than themselves. They also drag Christ's name through the mud and make it much more difficult for non-Christians to put their faith in Jesus.

So What's the Problem?

The summer after my junior year in college, I worked as an intern reporter at the *Journal Times* newspaper in Racine, Wisconsin. I had a great time and learned a lot, both about myself and about the news business. As I got ready to head back to school, I picked up a T-shirt created by the paper's advertising department. "Do it daily," it said in bold, block letters on one side. "Read the *Journal Times*," it said on the other.

Of course, I "got" the joke of the sexual double entendre. While I didn't feel too sure I ought to wear the T-shirt around campus, I consciously shelved my doubts. One day I wore the shirt to a journalism class designed for students who had served internships that summer. As soon as I walked in the room, my skeptical professor saw the shirt, raised his eyebrows, and in the sarcastic tone I had come to expect from him, said, "Steven—what a surprise. That's not the sort of message one might expect a *Christian* to promote."

Understand, I respected this man despite his gruff and often patronizing classroom manner. We had talked occasionally about my beliefs, and although he made no claim to follow Christ, he did like to mention how he had attended seminary in his younger years. I knew instantly what caused his amusement but pretended not to know.

"What do you mean?" I asked, innocently as I could.

"You know very well what I mean," he replied, pointing to the words emblazoned on my chest.

"What *about* the shirt?" I asked, looking down at the words. "It's just an advertisement to read the paper."

"Humph," he snorted, then turned away. While he said no more about it, I could tell in his eyes that I lost a little of his respect that day. He didn't share my beliefs, but he clearly wished that I would've had the guts to own my faith and not try to pretend that I didn't see how my behavior failed (at least in his mind) to live up to it.

That day I became a poster boy for Romans 2:24—and at the time I didn't even realize I was posing for a photo.

"You who preach against stealing," Paul asks, "do you steal? You who say that people should not commit adultery, do you commit adultery? You who abhor idols, do you rob temples? You who brag about the law, do you dishonor God by breaking the law? As it is written: *'God's name is blasphemed among the Gentiles because of you'*" (Romans 2:21–24).

While few nonbelievers are going to stand up and cheer you for living out your faith, many will respect you for it.

When my unbelieving prof turned away from me that day with a scoff in his throat, I was the one who instigated his "blasphemy." Not only had I chosen to wear something that my instructor considered at odds with the faith I claimed; I had then chosen to lie about my understanding of the problem. He knew it instantly—and so he scoffed. And in that way, God's name got blasphemed among the Gentiles . . . because of *me*.

A lot more is at stake in our lives of faith than we often realize. Non-Christians watch us, whether we remember it or not. More than once I have seen people turn away from Christ with sneering remarks like, "Hey, don't preach that stuff at *me*. You don't act any different than I do! You're no better than me. So, take your little message somewhere else."

It really doesn't have to be this way. While few nonbelievers are going to stand up and cheer you for living out your faith, many *will* respect you for it. And some day, you may just get the chance to introduce them to the same Jesus who is helping you to speak and act increasingly like His own heavenly Father.

His Very Own People

When God in His grace saves us, He saves for a purpose. He doesn't save us merely to keep us out of hell and give us a cool room in heaven. He saves us in order to make us into "soldiers of Christ."

Don't laugh! Most Bible scholars think that image is exactly what inspired the name "Christian." In Latin, the ancient tongue of the

Romans, the suffix -*iani* sometimes got added to a general's name to indicate the soldiers who served under him. Thus, a general named Galba commanded soldiers called *Galbiani*, "Galba's men."[2] In this way observers took the name *Christus* (Christ), added the -*iani* and came up with *Christiani*, "Christians." Christ's men. Christ's soldiers.

How do you become a soldier for Christ? How do you live as one of His men or women? You become a Christian by taking hold of God's grace and relying on it from start to finish. You don't start with grace and then forget about it until the skies break open and Christ appears in blinding light to take you home, along with the rest of His heavenly army. No. You "grow in grace," as Peter might say (2 Peter 3:18). If I were to choose a theme verse for this book, it would be this:

Those who say they live in God should live their lives as Christ did. (1 John 2:6 NLT)

Or to hear the same message from another perspective, consider the words of "the apostle of grace," Paul. He said that Jesus "gave his life to free us from every kind of sin, to cleanse us, and to make us his very own people, totally committed to doing what is right" (Titus 2:14 NLT).

That's what grace does: it gives us the *desire* and the *ability* to live as Christ did, to eagerly do what is right. Far from giving us the "right" or the "encouragement" to do what grieves God, grace sets our hearts on doing what most delights God's pure heart.

Grace certainly does *not* turn the sow's ear of sin into a silk purse of blessing, as we'll discover next.

2

A Good-Night Kiss for Twiggy

John Kohut and Roland Sweet have seen their share of stupid. As the authors of several books delighting in bizarre and absurd behavior, these two scour the world for reports of breathtaking human dim-wittedness.

A 1996 title, *Dumb, Dumber, Dumbest: True News of the World's Least Competent People*,[1] told how an eighteen-year old Englishman, Jordan Lazelle, had to be hospitalized after his pet scorpion bit him. One evening when Lazelle tried to give "Twiggy" its usual good-night kiss, the little beast grabbed his lip. When Lazelle opened his mouth in shock, the scorpion jumped inside and stung him several times on the tongue.

"It had never done that before," a startled (and hurting) Lazelle exclaimed.

Stupid? And then some. Unfortunately, you don't have to travel all the way to Merry Olde England to find similar accounts of world-class foolishness. Just a couple of months ago I read of a twenty-one-year-old man from Yacolt, Washington—a little farming community about twenty miles north of Portland, Oregon—whose pet rattlesnake rejected a little kiss from its owner.

"Snakes are attacked every day in the wild, and the first thing they see is a predator's eyes," explained one reptile expert. "They're going to bite."[2]

You think?

Matthew George didn't. He wound up in critical condition at a Portland hospital after his "pet" snake bit him on the lip. Doctors spared George's life only after a LifeFlight helicopter rushed him to the emergency room, where he received antivenin treatments.

Interesting, you might be thinking, *but what do foolish pet owners have to do with a book on grace?* Plenty, it turns out. Christians who misunderstand and misuse God's grace tend to make the same kinds of painful mistakes committed by Jordan and Matthew. They think they can make a pet out of a predator. Jordan chose a scorpion; Matthew chose a rattler; and many Christians choose sin. All of them mistakenly think that they can turn a wild and dangerous killer into a nice, little kitty or a sweet, playful doggy.

And then, without warning, the thing sinks its fangs into their faces.

It Looks Cool; Besides, It's Small

How do genuine believers get involved with killer kinds of sin? Probably the same way that Matthew George got hooked up with his rattlesnake. He picked it up on a trip to the Arizona desert three or four weeks before his brush with death. It looked intriguing and not so very dangerous. Besides, he caught a young snake, a small one—what harm could it do?

Many Christians follow a similar pattern when they start playing with their own "pet sins." The sin looks intriguing, exotic, different from what they're used to. It catches their attention and spikes their curiosity. They watch it for awhile, then nudge closer, and over time convince themselves that the thing can't possibly be nearly so hazardous as some say. Besides, isn't it just a little one? What harm could it do? *I'll just keep it as a pet,* they tell themselves. *I can certainly handle such a little thing!*

But even little beasts can kill.

The owner of Hart's Reptile World in Canby, Oregon, told the reporter researching the Matthew George story that a rattlesnake—even a small one—"is meant to bite. That's how it makes its living." Unlike adult rattlers, young snakes can't control the amount of venom that they inject into their victims. And George "sustained a life-threatening dose," according to the paramedic who called in the LifeFlight helicopter. Little ones can kill just as easily as big ones—sometimes more quickly.

Remember the story of Lot from the book of Genesis? Lot moved with his uncle, Abraham, from Ur to Canaan. But as the flocks and herds of both men grew, Abraham

Pet sins, even small ones, can bite your head off.

saw that he had to put some distance between him and his nephew. So he graciously gave Lot his choice of pasture land (13:8–9). Lot chose the area of "the cities of the plain," which at that time "was well watered, like the garden of the LORD" (v. 10). At first Lot only "pitched his tents *near* Sodom" (v. 12). In time Lot moved his whole family into the city (14:12), eventually becoming active in its politics (19:1).

Keep in mind that the Bible calls Lot a believer. The New Testament describes him as "a righteous man, who was distressed by the filthy lives of lawless men (for that righteous man, living among them day after day, was tormented in his righteous soul by the lawless deeds he saw and heard)" (2 Peter 2:7–8). Nevertheless, this genuine believer also felt a strong attraction to the pulsing rhythms of a wicked city. When God decided to destroy Sodom and its neighbors, Lot heeded a warning to flee—but he did so reluctantly. Ordered to obliterate the doomed communities, the angels told Lot to run to the mountains, but by that time Lot had grown too fond of city life. "No, my lords, please!" he told them. "I can't flee to the mountains; this disaster will overtake me, and I'll die. Look, here is a town near enough to run to, and it is small. Let me flee to it—it is very small, isn't it?" (19:18–20). The residents had named their town Zoar, which means "small."

Lot soon found out, however, that "small" and "appealing" don't necessarily mean either "wise" or "safe." Shortly after moving to Zoar, he took his surviving daughters and left town, "for he was afraid to stay" there (19:30).

Appealing? Sure. Attractive? In many ways. Small? Maybe so. But easy to handle? Not on your life. Pet sins, even small ones, can bite your head off.

It's Their Nature

It's smart to recall what the owner of Hart's Reptile World said about a rattlesnake: It's "meant to bite. That's how it makes its living." Sin is the same way. It bites by nature. You can't tame it, domesticate it, train it, or pacify it. You may think that you can make a pet out of it—especially some little, attractive sin—but at some point its pointy teeth will rip your flesh. Think that's a kitten you're playing with? It isn't. It's a bloodthirsty predator.

"Your enemy the devil prowls around like a roaring lion looking for someone to devour," warns the apostle Peter. (1 Peter 5:8)

Satan "was a murderer from the beginning," declared Jesus. (John 8:44)

The devil "holds the power of death," says the writer of Hebrews. (2:14)

"The sting of death is sin," proclaims the apostle Paul. (1 Corinthians 15:56)

Can they all be wrong? Can every one of them be seriously overreacting to something not nearly so deadly as all that? Or do they know something that can keep us from unnecessary trouble?

Wild and Totally Unpredictable

Scorpions and snakes can strike at anytime, without warning, even after long periods in which they appear harmless, even docile. Jordan Lazelle gave his scorpion dozens of good-night kisses before it finally drilled holes in his tongue. Matthew George kept his "pet" rattlesnake for three to four weeks without incident; it didn't strike until George decided to show off his little companion to a friend, Jim Roban.

"Even if George had handled the young rattlesnake safely other times," wrote the newspaper reporter, "each time can be a different story." A reptile expert agreed. "It's a wild animal and totally unpredictable," he said. "If they didn't bite or protect themselves, they'd be extinct."

Sin often works the same way. You choose to do something your gut tells you is wrong—and nothing bad happens. So a little later you do it again . . . and once more, nothing. Soon you begin to suspect that all those dire warnings about "the wages of sin" amount to little more than parental/biblical scare tactics. In time, the sin becomes a habit—a controlled, managed, "safe" sin, you think—and it ceases to concern you.

But sooner or later, it bites.

A friend of mine made this unpleasant discovery last year. I'll call her "Tara." As a young teen, Tara got pregnant outside of wedlock and gave up the baby for adoption, beginning a rough period that came to an end only after she committed her life to Christ. If anyone knew about "the wages of sin," Tara did, and she pledged never again to act on the whispers of the dark side. She joined a *Sin, like snakes and scorpions, sports an unpredictable side.* good church, read her Bible, made a lot of solid Christian friends, and even went on at least one summer missions trip. Eventually she got a great job with a respected Christian ministry. Life seemed fantastic.

And then she met "Jim," a smart and good-looking fellow Christian who strongly resembled Prince Charming. They started dating and soon these "thirty-somethings" appeared headed for marriage. Only one thing bothered Tara: her boyfriend insisted on a wide-open sexual relationship. First it was sex once in awhile; soon it was sex every night. He often stayed overnight at her place and constantly nudged her into bed, despite her vocal misgivings. Eventually Tara realized that their illicit sexual relationship displeased God and sabotaged their ability to genuinely get to know one another. She insisted that they redefine their relationship and set up appropriate boundaries—and Jeff exploded.

Weren't they adults? Didn't they have everything under control? Couldn't she see that their love made everything OK? Did she really want to deny him what he needed as a man? He just didn't see the problem. When Tara refused to budge, Jeff walked out.

Yet the controversy didn't end there. Over the next few months, Jeff made Tara's life a living hell. He made all sorts of serious public accusations against her and eventually dragged her into court, nearly succeeding in getting her jailed. Tara avoided prison, but to do so she spent thousands of dollars on lawyers and fines and came within a whisker of losing her job.

"Safe" sin? Ha! Sin, like snakes and scorpions, sports an unpredictable side. Someone who engages in habitual sin may dodge for a time the full consequences of that sin, but eventually the Lord *in His grace* withdraws His hand of protection and allows the sin to act on its natural instinct to bite. That's what happened with the Old Testament strongman, Samson.

While God used Samson to lessen the suffering of His oppressed people, Samson also indulged in frequent sexual sin. Time after time God spared Samson the full consequences of his offenses. But rather than change, Samson grew to depend on what he saw as his perpetual invincibility—until the day his God-given strength really left him. On that day, when his enemies surrounded him, the Bible says Samson "awoke from his sleep and thought, 'I'll go out as before and shake myself free.' But he did not know that the LORD had left him" (Judges 16:20).

Samson spent his last dreary days as a despised prisoner, his eyes gouged out and his body forced to do the labor of work animals.

God's grace does not provide anyone with invincible armor against the consequences of willful, habitual sin. And sometimes God Himself directs the enemy's arrows to pierce the chain mail He has so graciously provided.

How Fast It Moves!

While sin may sheathe its fangs for a time, it always strikes in the end. And its fast-acting poison often surprises its victims, their raised eyebrows wordlessly asking, "How could this *be?*"

Matthew George had a similar experience although in the physical realm. Had he not lived just two minutes away from paramedics, almost certainly he would have died. When help arrived on the scene about four minutes after the strike, George's lip looked a little swollen, nothing more. But a scant two minutes later, the venom spread up his face and down his neck and began to threaten his breathing. His lip swelled to five times its normal size, his ballooning cheeks and ears forced his eyes shut, and he began to drift in and out of consciousness. Paramedics had to insert a tube down his throat to keep his airway open. Before long, George's neck swelled to his chin.

"Had he lived out a little more," said one paramedic, "I strongly suspect he would not have survived."

Christians who play with sin usually feel surprised at how quickly the devil's venom spreads throughout their system. One moment all looks fine; the next, disaster. They never see it coming.

But they could! In His great grace, God gives us plenty of warnings about how quickly sin can turn and destroy us. Consider just two proverbs:

> He whose walk is blameless is kept safe,
> > but he whose ways are perverse will suddenly fall.
> (Proverbs 28:18)
> A man who remains stiff-necked after many rebukes
> > will suddenly be destroyed—without remedy.
> (Proverbs 29:1)

Once sin decides to sink its fangs into a victim, its venom spreads quickly and painfully. You feel as though you can't breathe. Your hands tremble. You stutter. You find it hard to stand, let alone walk. And the agony just grows and grows. King David, a man after God's own heart, nevertheless used the following aching words to describe his own condition while he tried to hide a sin he deliberately chose:

> When I kept silent,
> > my bones wasted away
> > through my groaning all day long.
> For day and night
> > your hand was heavy upon me;
> my strength was sapped
> > as in the heat of summer. (Psalm 32:3–4)

Sin may not choose to open its piercing jaws for some time. It may allow believers to enjoy its secret pleasures for days or months or even years before it rattles its tail. But when it shows its teeth and plants them in human flesh, be sure that its deadly poison follows soon after.

A Concern for Public Safety

One of the saddest aspects of Matthew George's near-death experience is that it never had to happen. The attempt to kiss a rattler is not only stupid; in Washington, it is clearly illegal. The state has laws against keeping such dangerous animals as pets. Why? To protect the public from itself.

Dennis Davidson, chief investigator for Clark County Animal Control, explained that state law prohibits the unauthorized entry of nonnative animals, such as the Arizona rattler that bit George. Those who want to keep such creatures must annually pay a one-hundred-dollar license fee and submit an application demonstrating that they have appropriate training and can meet minimum standards of care. George ignored both requirements.

In the spiritual realm, the grace of God does not mean that our heavenly Father must exempt us from suffering the consequences of our intentionally chosen sin. In fact, it was the grace of God that moved Him to give us the Bible, which instructs us to reject sin, not coddle it. Just as the state of Washington tries to protect its citizens by prohibiting them from importing dangerous nonnative species, so God tries to protect His children by prohibiting them from trying to make a pet out of the lethal viper of sin.

The apostle Paul probably had God's fatherly nature in mind when he wrote, "For everything that was written in the past was written to teach us, so that through endurance and the encouragement of the Scriptures we might have hope" (Romans 15:4). God does not tell us to refrain from certain things to irritate or frustrate us, but to keep us from harm.

You still want to kiss a rattler? OK, go ahead. But I hope you like the swollen neck look.

So, Who's Responsible?

I have a friend, a Christian, who repeatedly makes foolish and unbiblical choices and then blames God for the disastrous results. "God always seems to do this to me," he wrote in one recent e-mail after yet another unwise decision blew up in his face.

But is such a conclusion fair? Does the grace of God really mean that He must allow us to do whatever harebrained and evil thing pops into our heads, and then make sure that everything comes out OK? Must He plummet on the Grace-O-Meter when He permits us to suffer the consequences for doing the very thing He instructed us to avoid? I don't think so, and I believe the owner of Hart's Reptile World would agree with me.

This most sensible woman placed the blame for George's unfortunate run-in with the rattlesnake squarely on the shoulders of Matthew George himself. "Obviously that person shouldn't have had that snake to begin with," she said. And the reptile expert quoted earlier in the newspaper story seconded the motion. "So who's responsible?" he asked. "The one with the bigger brain."

(Chuck Shepherd, writer of "News of the Weird," in telling this story added something unkind, "but he did not say which one he thought that was."[3])

> *You have a brain. Use it. Keep your lips away from anything with venom and fangs.*

If sin in the spiritual world is like a rattlesnake in the physical world, then who should we blame when things go disastrously wrong during a botched snake kissing? If no one blames God for Matthew George's brush with the undertaker, then why should anyone blame God for a supposed lack of "grace" when their own sin pumps venom into their veins?

You have a brain. Use it. Keep your lips away from anything with venom and fangs.

Meeting Its End

One sad postscript should be added to the tale of the rattlesnake that refused its keeper's kiss. After the serpent bit its keeper on the lip, George's friend, Jim Roban, retaliated by cutting off the snake's head.

While Roban's decisive action truly can be considered a tragedy for the guiltless animal—after all, the snake did only what a wild creature of its kind ought to do in similar circumstances—at the same time it provides a great example of what any smart believer ought to do when confronted with sin.

Kill it. Cut off its head. Exterminate the thing and then beat a hasty retreat.

While we'll take a closer look at this extreme strategy in a bit (see chap. 14), for now it's enough to remember the apostle Paul's take on it: "Now those who belong to Christ Jesus have crucified the flesh with its passions and desires" (Galatians 5:24 NASB). To "crucify," of course, means "to kill." And it's the only sure way to keep a viper's poison out of your system.

Same Song, Second (or Third?) Verse

I know that some might consider all this talk of snakes and venom and sin and consequences quite overblown. Over the top. Blown way out of proportion. And I start to think, *Maybe they're right.*

But then I read about Eric VanNorde.

VanNorde, twenty-nine years old back in May 2002, had to be airlifted to Jacobi Medical Center in the Bronx, New York, "because his snake, which he reportedly told authorities he was trying to kiss, bit him first."[4]

Ah, yes. The old "kiss the poisonous snake" routine (this time, with an eastern diamondback, considered the "most dangerous of poisonous snakes in the United States"). Just when you think, *Nobody will ever try that again,* somebody does.

So let me leave you with a warning limerick:

> Whenever you play with a sin,
> I beg you to please, Think Again.
> For that snake will bite quick
> And leave you real sick—
> Or with (maybe) a sad next-of-kin.

3

Wrong Turns

I have a lousy sense of direction. I've lived in the same area now for twenty years, but all it takes for me to get lost is to travel down an unfamiliar street from an unusual direction. Same landmarks, same buildings, same road, same traffic patterns—and yet I have no idea where I am.

Back in seminary I got lost so frequently that I tried a simple experiment. I kept a one-month log to track all the times I came to an unfamiliar crossing. After turning left or right, I would record whether I had chosen the right or wrong direction. I felt confident that at the end of the month, I'd see that I chose correctly just about as often as I took a wrong turn.

Not quite. At the end of the test, I found that I had made the wrong turn more than *90 percent* of the time.

Armed with data like this, you might think that I'd just head the opposite way my gut told me to go. But I just couldn't get myself to do it.

In the past year life has become a little easier for me. My wife and I bought a car equipped with a navigation system. Before I start out for an unfamiliar destination, I plug in the address and my car tells me, quite literally, how to get there. Almost without fail it gets me where I need to be—which is a lot more than I can say for my own miserable efforts.

Theological Wrong Turns

As bad as geographical wrong turns make me feel, they pale in comparison to theological wrong turns. Usually it's not very hard to recover from a geographical wrong turn. It may cost me a few minutes but ordinarily not much more. Theological wrong turns, however, can set a person back for years, even a lifetime. Theological wrong turns can lead to long-term disappointment, agonizing confusion, and worse.

His college buddies called him "Herff" and knew him as "a glad-handing, beanie-wearing freshman."[1] He helped lead an a cappella choir, sat on the college judiciary council, and actively worked with the campus association of prospective Presbyterian ministers. After college, Herff enrolled at the Union Theological Seminary of Virginia and took courses on the Old and New Testaments, theology, and practical ministry. He quickly dropped out, however, to pursue his interest in music. He took a position as the director of music at the First Presbyterian Church in Gastonia, North Carolina, and over the next twenty years moved to various states where he worked several jobs.

Somewhere in those years, Herff took some seriously wrong theological turns. He met a nurse named Bonnie Lu Nettles, "and the two discovered a mutual interest in astrology and reincarnation and came to believe that they were the earthly incarnations of aliens."[2] Herff and Nettles began roaming the country and preaching about unidentified flying objects, claiming that alien spacecraft offered a gateway to a better world. Eventually Herff convinced thirty-eight followers not only to join his Heaven's Gate cult, but to commit mass suicide in the belief that a spaceship traveling with a passing comet would retrieve their souls and take them to a fabulous higher plane of existence. And so in late March 1997, police entering a million-dollar home in Rancho Santa Fe, California, discovered the bodies of thirty-nine men and women who willingly followed Marshall Herff Applewhite into oblivion.

Not all theological wrong turns, of course, end in such headline-grabbing disaster. Most don't. A friend of mine has struggled for the last decade with strong feelings of discouragement, fear, deep dissatisfaction with life, and frequent hopelessness. He never joined a Heaven's Gate-type cult and throughout the last ten years has attended strong, Bible-centered churches. Yet somewhere along the way he took a wrong theological turn. Much of his dark mood can be traced to a defective belief that if he just acted like a good little boy and kept his nose fairly clean God would make all of his dreams come true. Life hasn't turned out that way for my friend, and only after a decade of exhausting disappointment has he begun to realize that the problem may lie with his own unrealistic (and unbiblical) expectations.

Unfortunately, we don't usually know that we've taken a theological wrong turn until our surroundings look vastly different from what we expected. We thought we were heading to Malibu and instead find ourselves in Toad Suck, Arkansas.

In this chapter I want to try to help you stay on track in your Christian journey by warning you ahead of time about a few theological wrong turns that often lead to warped forms of grace. They've become increasingly common and have sent thousands of believers down dark, dead-end roads. The good news is that if you stay alert, you don't have to join them.

An Uncomfortable Question

"Does God blush?"

A former colleague of mine asked that question sometime ago, and I've wondered about it ever since. At first I agreed with Mark Twain, who famously wrote, "Man is the only animal that blushes, or needs to." People blush because they feel ashamed or embarrassed by something they do or because of an encounter that offends their modesty. Because God never does anything that would make Him feel ashamed or embarrassed, and because (so far as I can tell) He has no need of modesty, I thought the answer to the question was "no."

But the more I thought about it, the more I wondered. Then one day I read Hebrews 11, the Bible's "Hall of Faith" chapter, and my questions multiplied. That passage describes Christians as "aliens and strangers on earth" (v. 13) and declares that, "Therefore God is not ashamed to be called their God" (v. 16). If I follow the writer's logic, he seems to be saying several things:

- The famous believers in this passage all lived by faith;

- Living by faith means that you base your life on God's promises;
- Depending on God's promises gets you "looking" and "longing" for "a better country—a heavenly one" (v. 16);
- Those who live in this way give no reason for God to feel ashamed of them.

So far so good. God "is not ashamed to be called their God," and so God really doesn't blush after all. End of question.

Or is it?

One little word threw me: "therefore." The appearance of this word suggests that God feels no shame in being called the God of faith-filled people for one primary reason: they long for a better country, a heavenly one. They never allow themselves to get too comfortable. They never forget that, as Job said, "Naked I came from my mother's womb, and naked I will depart" (Job 1:21); or as Paul put it, "For we brought nothing into the world, and we can take nothing out of it" (1 Timothy 6:7). They work hard for the betterment of this world, but they consider themselves "aliens and strangers."

> *Could it be that the Lord of glory feels embarrassed by the behavior of some members of His family?*

But what if things were different? What if these believers *didn't* long for a better country? What if they *didn't* desire a heavenly home more than they enjoyed their current, earthly one? What if they felt completely satisfied with all their clothes and houses and food and toys and trinkets? Would God feel ashamed of them *then*?

The writer doesn't answer—and his silence makes me wonder. Maybe God really *does* blush.

Is it possible that the God of the universe feels ashamed of some of us, at least some of the time? Could it be that the Lord of glory feels embarrassed by the behavior of some members of His family? If we had a giant telescope that could bring the throne room of heaven into sharp focus, might we see God's shining face suddenly redden in front of His holy angels when one of us on earth began acting in ways not much different from those who lack any hope of heaven? Does God ever blush over the conduct of some of His kids?

To tell the truth, I don't like the question. In some ways, I'm glad the Bible doesn't seem to directly answer it. I know the Scripture says that my sin always displeases and even angers God, but there's something about the Lord blushing over my behavior that makes me squirm. I don't want Him to feel embarrassed by me. I don't want to think of Him blushing in front of one of His angels and saying, "Well, yes, Steve does belong to me. That's right, I mean *that* Steve. It may not look like it right now, but he really will be here soon. In fact, he'll live just a few doors down from you."

Does God Smile or Wink?

Many of us take a wrong turn in our view of God. We hear so often that He loves us (true!) and that He wants to spend eternity with us (true!) and that He sent His Son to die for us (true!) that we begin to think that He just winks at our "mistakes" and "misjudgments" and "missteps" (false!). We forget that God takes sin seriously—all sin, including that of Christians—and that both in the past and in the future He promises to deal with it decisively.

As much as I love verses like John 3:16—"For God so loved the world that he gave his one and only Son, that whoever believes in him shall not perish but have eternal life"—I wonder if it isn't past time to mull over some equally valid verses.

I think of what the psalmist said about God: "He will not always strive *with us,* nor will He keep *His anger* forever" (Psalm 103:9 NASB).

I remember Acts 5 and what happened to two members of the church whom the apostle Peter said had "lied" to God. On the spot they both fell down dead, and "great fear seized the whole church and all who heard about these events" (v. 11).

I think about 1 Corinthians 10 and the warnings the apostle Paul gave his church friends. He reminded the Corinthians that "God was not pleased" with most of the Israelites and that "their bodies were scattered over the desert" (v. 5). He recalled that 23,000 Israelites died in a single day because of sexual immorality (v. 8); that others "tested" the Lord and died from painful snakebites (v. 9); that still others grumbled about God's care and died at the hands of "the destroying angel" (v. 10). And I take note that he said, "these things oc-

curred as examples to keep us from setting our hearts on evil things
as they did. . . . These things happened to them as examples and were
written down as warnings for us" (vv. 6, 11).

I think about Peter and his sobering words to fellow believers:
"For it is time for judgment to begin with the family of God; and if it
begins with us, what will the outcome be for those who do not obey
the gospel of God?" (1 Peter 4:17).

Yes, God is love (where would we be if He weren't?). Yes, God is
patient (how would we come to faith otherwise?). Yes, God is gracious (why else would He send His Son to the cross?). But don't get the
wrong idea. Don't take a wrong turn. Never even think about "sinning
now and asking forgiveness later." If that's what you're counting on,
you're about to take a disastrously wrong turn. And you won't like
where the detour puts you.

My Good Buddy

A pop group whose music I still like churned out a hit song several years ago featuring the frequent refrain, "Jesus is just all right
with me."

While I'm sure the good Lord appreciates the group's giddy en-
dorsement, I can't help but wonder if too many of us have taken the
lyric just a little too far. In our zeal to embrace Jesus as one of us, as
a brother, as a human being with skin and hair and fingernails and
maybe even acne, sometimes we make Him into little more than My
Good Buddy.

This Jesus-as-My-Good-Buddy walks around ancient Palestine
with a perpetual grin on His lips. He loves holding babies and going
to parties. He knows just when to put a comforting arm around a discouraged friend's shoulder. He speaks often of God's love and lights up
whenever He describes heaven. He knows He has to die for the sins of
the world, and that saddens Him, but He's willing to do it because He
thinks His friends are so cool. He can't wait to welcome them to the
Pearly Gates, where together they'll all enjoy a fiesta that never ends.

Does that last paragraph sound a little cynical to you? I hope not
because most of it is absolutely true. Jesus did love holding babies and
going to parties. He did know how to comfort a discouraged friend.
He did often speak of God's love. He did unveil some beautiful pearls

about heaven. And He did feel great anguish over the approaching ordeal of His crucifixion. All of that is absolutely true.

But Jesus was so much more than that! How could He be anything less, since the Bible makes it clear that He is God Himself (Hebrews 1:3)? The same Jesus who spoke of heaven also spoke (even more frequently) about hell. The same Jesus who loved holding babies also told mothers to weep for their infants and predicted that the day would come when they would wish they had never given birth (Luke 23:28–29). The same Jesus who put a comforting hand on a drooping shoulder could also call a close friend "Satan" and could repeatedly call His most devoted followers "foolish" and ask them things like, "are you so dull?" and "where is your faith?" (Matthew 4:10; Luke 24:25; Matthew 15:16; Luke 8:25).

It is wonderfully true that the Bible calls Jesus the Good Shepherd, the Lamb of God, our brother and friend, and the Savior of the world (John 10:11; 1:29; Hebrews 2:11; John 15:15; 1 John 4:14). I love all of these titles because each one teaches me something delightful about Jesus Christ. But the Scripture also calls Jesus the Son of God, the Lord of glory, the ruler of God's creation, the Alpha and the Omega, the King of kings and Lord of lords (Hebrews 4:14; 1 Corinthians 2:8; Revelation 3:14; 22:13; 19:16). I love these titles equally and relish the fuller picture they paint of my amazing Savior.

We take a wrong turn when we think of Jesus merely as My Good Buddy. The true Savior not only encourages; He rebukes. He not only teaches; He commands. He not only comforts; He terrifies. He not only lives; He dies . . . and lives once more, never to die again.

This Savior freely and gladly associates with thieves and drunks and mercenaries and prostitutes and embezzlers and blowhards and all the riff-raff that more proper society emphatically excludes. Yet He refuses merely to be a friend. He did not come to earth to make nice. Remember, this is the guy who told His associates, "Do not suppose that I have come to bring peace to the earth. I did not come to bring peace, but a sword" (Matthew 10:34). Immediately after Jesus rescues a woman obviously guilty of adultery (a capital crime in Jesus' day), He tells her, "Go now and leave your life of sin" (John 8:11). A Good Buddy would have said, "Go now and live however you please." But Jesus is much, much more than that.

Saved and Sassy

"I know I probably shouldn't get drunk," Andy admitted, "but I really like the buzz. It helps me loosen up and have fun." He paused, shifted uneasily in his chair, then continued. "Besides," he said, "even if it is wrong, I'm saved. I'm going to heaven. Jesus will forgive me." Then he smiled.

Andy has taken a wrong turn that, these days, looks more like a major thoroughfare. It's hard to recognize you're going the wrong way when you're sailing down the middle of a huge convoy.

Later in this book we'll take a look at how God intends grace to lead us to obedience (see chap. 9), but for now I'd like to briefly consider a defective—yet wildly popular—version of salvation. This brand of salvation says that, "Since I'm saved, I can sin however I want, because God already has forgiven me." It feels right at home with a warped view that insists, "Grace allows me to sin without fear of serious consequences."

There's a true half to this mistaken belief. The Bible does teach that those who are "in Christ Jesus" have received eternal life. Jesus explicitly says of these people, "I give them eternal life, and they shall never perish; no one can snatch them out of my hand. My Father, who has given them to me, is greater than all; no one can snatch them out of my Father's hand" (John 10:28–29). To make it even more clear, Jesus declares, "I tell you the truth, whoever hears my word and believes him who sent me has eternal life and will not be condemned; he has crossed over from death to life" (John 5:24).

So does this mean that once you've asked Jesus to be your Savior you can do whatever you want and still be OK? Well, yes and no. It depends on what you mean by "do whatever you want."

The Bible never imagines a genuinely "saved" person who still eagerly wants to sin. The Bible assumes that when you come to Christ, your "tastes" gradually begin to change. Before you became a Christian, your spiritual taste buds drove you to crave heaping cupfuls of the *sin du jour*—illicit sex, stolen cookies, illegal drugs, whatever. But after Christ came into your life and His Holy Spirit made your body His home, something happened to those spiritual taste buds. They began to yearn for other delicacies. What used to give you a buzz now gives you the blahs. What once gave you a thrill now makes you feel guilty. Usually this change doesn't occur overnight, but it always happens wherever genuine conversion takes place. And if it doesn't begin to happen somewhere along the way, something major has gone wrong.

The apostle Peter claimed that a genuine Christian "does not live the rest of his earthly life for evil human desires, but rather for the will of God." Why? Because, Peter says, "you have spent enough time in the past doing what pagans choose to do—living in debauchery, lust, drunkenness, orgies, carousing and detestable idolatry" (1 Peter 4:2–3).

Salvation is not free fire insurance that allows you to play with matches. Salvation is a miraculous rescue from a burning house that gives you a healthy respect for fire and a deep desire to point others to the emergency exits.

The apostle Paul said essentially the same thing. In perhaps the greatest passage in the Bible on this topic, he wrote, "As for you, you were dead in your transgressions and sins, in which you used to live when you followed the ways of this world and of the ruler of the kingdom of the air, the spirit who is now at work in those who are disobedient. All of us also lived among them at one time, gratifying the cravings of our sinful nature and following its desires and thoughts. Like the rest, we were by nature objects of wrath" (Ephesians 2:1–3).

But then something remarkable happened. God stepped in and transformed some spiritual taste buds, and their owners began craving another kind of life, another sort of lifestyle. Paul said it like this: "But because of his great love for us, God, who is rich in mercy, made us alive with Christ even when we were dead in transgressions—it is by grace you have been saved. And God raised us up with Christ. . . . For we are God's workmanship, created in Christ Jesus to do good works, which God prepared in advance for us to do" (vv. 4–6, 10).

Salvation is not free fire insurance that allows you to play with matches. Salvation is a miraculous rescue from a burning house that gives you a healthy respect for fire and a deep desire to point others to the emergency exits.

So what if you've "prayed the prayer" but you still have every intention of playing with those matches? Then the apostle of grace has another word for you: "Once you were alienated from God and were enemies in your minds because of your evil behavior," he writes. "But now he has reconciled you by Christ's physical body through death to present you holy in his sight, without blemish and free from accusation—*if you continue in your faith, established and firm, not moved from the hope held out in the gospel*" (Colossians 1:21–23). Notice the big little word "if." *If* you continue in your faith.

And just how do you "continue in your faith"? Paul answers that one, too: "First to those in Damascus, then to those in Jerusalem and in all Judea, and to the Gentiles also, I preached that they should repent and turn to God and *prove their repentance by their deeds*" (Acts 26:20). You continue in your faith by allowing your faith to produce the kind of actions that please God. More and more you follow the lead of your new spiritual taste buds and begin to gorge on food that smells of heaven.

Your deeds don't save you, nor do they play even the smallest role in keeping your salvation; but they *do* prove your repentance. And without that proof, Paul might say of us what he said about some other professing believers: "They claim to know God, but by their actions they deny him. They are detestable, disobedient and unfit for doing anything good" (Titus 1:16).

Remember, that's the apostle of grace speaking. That's the man who wrote more about grace than anyone else in the Bible. And he seems to be saying, "Watch out for wrong turns on the way to salvation. Don't go flying down the wrong highway just because a lot of others are moving in that direction."

Believe the Navigator

I got lost the other day. I thought I knew where I was going, but several wrong turns in a row got me hopelessly disoriented.

And then I remembered my on-board navigator.

I don't know why I didn't plug in the address as soon as I took my seat behind the wheel, but I didn't. I probably thought I knew the right directions well enough. No doubt I thought I knew the lay of the land. Ha!

So I pulled off to the side of the road and typed in the target address. After a few seconds of comparing my GPS-determined position with its DVD map, my navigator told me precisely how to get to where I wanted to be. And just a couple of minutes later, I drove right up to the front door.

Don't waste your time wandering around theological back alleys. Grace is a fabulous thing, but if you fail to engage your Navigator—the Holy Spirit as He guides you to a healthy interpretation of Scripture—you may well take a wrong turn that gets you frustratingly lost.

So avoid the wandering bit. Stay on the right track. And arrive safely at God's picnic, where you can enjoy a meaty, robust grace that sticks to your ribs and satisfies those new spiritual taste buds of yours.

(But do beware the marshmallows. They come from another campground, and we'll talk about them next.)

4

Marshmallow Grace

*H*ave you ever gone camping or sat around a campfire when someone broke out the graham crackers, chocolate, and marshmallows and suggested that it might be a good time to make a few s'mores? Everyone scrambles to find long, sharp sticks and quickly skewers two or three sugary, white puffballs. Before long, the sweet smell of golden-brown marshmallows (or more often, blackened and crispy ones) fills the air. And very soon, melted chocolate and gooey white stuff starts sticking to your smiling face.

You can't have a true s'more without chocolate and graham crackers; but those ingredients, delicious as they are, don't make up the essence of the genuine article. Purists define real s'mores by the presence of toasted marshmallows. Without golden brown marshmallows, you just can't have a genuine s'more.

Most of us deeply savor toasted marshmallows. We like them gooey and we like them warm. We glory in their sweetness, in their sugary aroma, and in their slippery texture. We love the way they stick to our fingers and the way they slide down our throats. Some of us love them so much that we think, *Life should be more like a s'more—warm, soft, sweet, and comforting.*

And that's exactly where we can make a huge mistake.

Why? Because, very often, life *isn't* warm, soft, sweet, and comforting—and so we dream up ways to imagine that it is (or that it should be). If we count ourselves Christians, we may do this by adopting a warped version of grace. Somehow we convince ourselves that "being gracious" and "being nice" are the same thing.

They aren't.

The Right Starting Place

Marshmallow grace sees the world in soft, pastel colors. It leans toward rounded shapes and curvy figures and either avoids or denies the existence of sharp, jagged lines. It prefers slippers to hiking boots and an overstuffed chair to a walking stick.

Marshmallow grace finds it impossible to believe that God could ever act in rough or severe ways. It cannot comprehend a God who could both love and discipline His children at the same. It tends to minimize His "hard" side and emphasize His "soft" side, and frequently tries to put a wide gap between the "judgmental" God of the Old Testament and the "gracious" God of the New Testament.

In other words, marshmallow grace worships a nice God—but not at all the God of the Bible.

The Bible insists that only one true God exists, and that only one has ever existed or ever will exist. This God never changes; He is the same yesterday, today, and forever (Malachi 3:6; Hebrews 13:8). He did not get "nicer" after the birth of His Son at Bethlehem.

At all times, this God remains infinitely loving and boundlessly holy, eternally gracious and forever just. He does not trade off His holiness for His love or bounce back and forth between His justice and His mercy, depending on His current mood. In God, both "kindness and sternness" exist equally at the same time (Romans 11:22)—and it is when we forget this that our faith begins to go marshmallow on us.

We can tell when this happens because we begin to equate "soft" with "good" and "hard" with "bad." We start to believe that the main ingredient in grace is pure extract of nice. And soon we lose a central element of our faith that enables us to give hope to a hurting world.

Is the Gospel Ever Hard?

A few years back, I received a memo from a friend who worked with a well-known Christian author. This author (we'll call him "Bill") had written a book for adults that my friend thought might be adapted for a younger audience. When my friend asked an unidentified writer whether he had any interest in redoing the book for a teen audience, the man responded with an emphatic "no." Then the writer attached a long review explaining why he had to decline the job.

My friend sent me the memo to get my perspective because in the past I had worked with Bill. Of course, I have no problem with anyone turning down a project for any number of reasons. I have often done so myself. But the more of the memo I read, the more irritated I became. Time after time, it seemed to me, the reviewer had objected to Bill's book out of a staunch commitment to marshmallow grace. So I wrote a lengthy response in return and sent it to my friend.

I won't bore you with the whole thing (when I get riled over issues like this, I've been known to shoot off long letters; my record is seventeen single-spaced pages), but I would like to reproduce my reaction to a portion of the reviewer's comments.

So now the reviewer lectures us that it's inappropriate to use fear as a motivator? Says who? While this mythical "conflict" between Old and New Testaments gets a lot of play these days, it remains as baseless as ever. The reviewer is simply wrong that "the New Testament writers chose not to use these tactics." Let's see: last I knew, it was Jesus who said, "Unless you repent, you too will all perish" (Luke 13:3, 5—New Testament, right?). Wasn't it Jesus (in the New Testament) who said, "anyone who says, 'You fool!' will be in danger of the fire of hell" (Matthew 5:22)? Perhaps someone should have informed the Lord that He erred in using "intimidation" when He said things like, "That servant who knows his master's will and does not get ready or does not do what his master wants will be beaten with many blows. But the one who does not know and does things deserving punishment will be beaten with few blows. From everyone who has been given much, much will be demanded; and from the one who has been entrusted with much, much more will be asked" (Luke 12:47–48).

It would be spectacularly easy to find similar statements from Luke and Paul and Peter and James and John and the unnamed writer to the Hebrews ("If we deliberately keep on sinning after we have received the knowledge of the truth, no sacrifice for sins is left, but only a *fearful* expectation of judgment and of raging fire that will consume the enemies of God. . . . It is a *dreadful* thing to fall into the hands of the living God," Hebrews 10:26–27, 31). A mushy understanding of "grace" has done a lot to produce the egocentric, casual Christianity that slouches in the nation's pews today.

Am I greatly mistaken, or do many people today really think the main ingredient in God's grace is toasted marshmallows?

As you can see, I've been thinking about "marshmallow grace" for some time. And I believe that it leads unavoidably to serious problems for the church and for individual Christians. Let me suggest just a few of them.

Compassion or Mistaken Tenderness?

True compassion seeks the *long-term* welfare of those who suffer, not merely an immediate easing of pain. It is possible to treat a symptom and end up making the disease worse. Authentic compassion works for the long haul; therefore, it may decide that it cannot rush to alleviate current pain.

> *Do many people today really think the main ingredient in God's grace is toasted marshmallows?*

There's a big difference between compassion and mistaken tenderness, just as there's a big difference between grace and niceness. Sometimes, in order to be truly gracious—that is, in order to lovingly help a person move solidly toward health and happiness—you have to refuse to act in a way that will immediately reduce the pain. It may be that very pain that will nudge the person to seek a better long-term situation; to alleviate it too soon would only keep the individual in permanent agony. It might seem a nicer course of action to lessen the pain, but it wouldn't be gracious.

Suppose you asked your parents for permission to go on a spring break trip to Cancun with some friends. Suppose your parents knew that the adults who agreed to chaperone actually intended to leave to visit Acapulco. So on that basis your Mom and Dad turn down your request—and you fly into a rage.

"That's not fair! I already bought some beach clothes! Everybody else is still going! How can you say you love me?"

At that moment, would your parents seem "nice"? Hardly. Nice parents would certainly let their kids go. Gracious parents, however, surely would not. Gracious parents want the best for their sons and daughters and will willingly exchange some short-term fun for a long-term good.

Discipline or Absolute Acceptance?

Many of us have a hard time seeing how the Bible's guidelines concerning church discipline—1 Corinthians 5:1–13 comes to mind—square with other scriptural commands to accept and love one another. After all, some of these guidelines seem pretty harsh. *If we're all sinners*, we wonder, *then how can any of us presume to discipline others?*

Grace might answer in the words of Paul. Regarding the young Christian who openly slept with his stepmother, the apostle wrote: "hand this man over to Satan, so that the sinful nature may be destroyed and his spirit saved on the day of the Lord" (1 Corinthians 5:5).

Wow. I confess I don't know for sure what Paul meant by "hand this man over to Satan," but whatever it is, it doesn't sound "nice." He may have meant nothing more than what he explicitly said a little later: "purge the evil from among you" (quoting Deuteronomy 17:7 and several other places in the Old Testament). He may have meant that a Christian excluded from Christian fellowship forfeits the divine protection that God grants His church.

The point that we must not miss, however, is that Paul—the apostle of grace, the man whom God used more than any other to explain and promote the Good News of salvation through faith in Christ—directed his Corinthian friends to take what seems like harsh action in response to the blatant sin of one of their own.

Nice? No way. But gracious? You bet. Apparently it was this very action that later prompted the young believer to change his ways. So Paul wrote in a subsequent letter, "The punishment inflicted on him by the majority is sufficient for him. Now instead, you ought to forgive and comfort him, so that he will not be overwhelmed by excessive sorrow. I urge you, therefore, to reaffirm your love for him" (2 Corinthians 2:6–8).

I'll take grace over nice any day.

Fear or Reverence?

During my last year of seminary I had to write an in-depth technical paper on a topic of my choosing in order to demonstrate that I had achieved an acceptable level of linguistic competence. (I had to or I wouldn't graduate.)

Each of the twenty or so students had to present a paper to the class on an assigned date. After every presentation, the professor encouraged us to ask questions—to grill the one in the spotlight, in other words. No student before me received more than two or three queries, and those few came painfully, as if the questioner had thought, *Well, if no one else is going to ask anything, I suppose I should.*

Yet after I finished my presentation, every hand in the room shot up.

Did the response surprise me? Not really. I expected something like it, although not because of my topic: "The Fear of God As Developed in the Book of Hebrews." I anticipated an onslaught of questions because of the conclusion I drew, namely, that the "fear of God" in Hebrews is not mere reverence or awe, but genuine, teeth-chattering, knee-knocking terror.

These days, most Christians don't see it that way. A God who inspires terror, even "holy terror," in His children, simply can't be a God of grace. And so we take a healthy word like "fear" and dilute it into something a good deal less muscular, like "awe" or "reverence" or "respect" or "veneration."

And yet, there stands Moses in chapter 12 of Hebrews, the sweat pouring down his trembling face and his knees ready to buckle. He had approached God Almighty on a flaming Mount Sinai, not for judgment but to seal a permanent deal between the Lord and Israel—and yet the "sight was so terrifying that Moses said, 'I am trembling with fear'" (Hebrews 12:21).

But that's Old Testament stuff, someone thinks. *Things have changed!* Yes, they have. Thank God! The writer of Hebrews takes pains to announce how greatly things have changed. We do not come to a fiery mountain to receive tablets of stone, but we come "to Mount Zion, to the heavenly Jerusalem, the city of the living God. You have come to thousands upon thousands of angels in joyful assembly, to the church of the firstborn, whose names are written in heaven. You have come to God, the judge of all men, to the spirits of righteous men made perfect, to Jesus the mediator of a new covenant, and to the sprinkled blood that speaks a better word than the blood of Abel" (Hebrews 12:22–24).

And yet . . . not everything has changed. Did God terrify Moses by shaking the mountain? In the future He promises to "shake not only the earth but also the heavens" (12:26). So the urgent warning sounds: "See to it that you do not refuse him who speaks. If they did not escape when they refused him who warned them on earth, how much less will we, if we turn away from him who warns us from heaven?" (12:25). The writer ends this section of his letter with some sobering words: "Therefore, since we are receiving a kingdom that cannot be shaken, let us be thankful, and so worship God acceptably with reverence and awe, for our 'God is a consuming fire'" (12:28–29).

The Greek words translated "reverence" and "awe" are more literally rendered "fear" (*eulabeias*) and "fear" (*deous*),[1] although such a translation obviously comes up short. It seems as though the author wants to ensure, through repetition, that we never slip into thinking that God's grace "tames" Him from a lion into a house cat. In fact, the phrase "let us be thankful" is more literally, "let us have *grace*"—demonstrating that a strong emphasis on grace never loses its holy fear of God Almighty.

One celebrated commentator writes about this passage, "the writer emphasizes that God is not to be trifled with. We can be so taken up with the love and compassion of God that we overlook his implacable opposition to all evil. The wrath of God is not a popular subject today, but it looms large in biblical teaching. We overlook this wrath only at our peril."[2]

So what does it mean to "fear" a loving and gracious God? How can we fear Him and yet not be afraid of Him? Another writer says, "the kind of fear that we should have toward God is whatever is left of fear when we have a sure hope in the midst of it."[3] And then he gives a helpful picture:

> Suppose you were exploring an unknown Greenland glacier in the dead of winter. Just as you reach a sheer cliff with a spectacular view of miles of jagged ice and mountains of snow, a terrible storm breaks in. The wind is so strong

that the fear rises in your heart that it might blow you over the cliff. But in the midst of the storm you discover a cleft in the ice where you can hide. Here you feel secure. But, even though secure, the awesome might of the storm rages on, and you watch it with a kind of trembling pleasure as it surges out across the distant glaciers. Not everything we call fear vanishes from your heart; only the life-threatening part. There remains the trembling, the awe, the wonder, the feeling that you would never want to tangle with such a storm or be the adversary of such a power.

And so it is with God. The fear of God is what is left of the storm when you have a safe place to watch right in the middle of it. Hope turns fear into a trembling and peaceful wonder; and fear takes everything trivial out of hope and makes it earnest and profound. The terrors of God make the pleasures of His people intense. The fireside fellowship is all the sweeter when the storm is howling outside the cottage.[4]

There may be no place for fear in an ocean of nice, but grace dives in it and makes the plunge refreshingly sweet.

Sucking the Life Out

Grace and niceness are not the same thing, anymore than toasted marshmallows and a grilled sirloin provide the same eating experience. So why don't we abandon the Sta-Puft life and bite into some steak?

For one thing, too often we've immersed ourselves in activities and habits that suck the life out of our souls. We may know they're wrong, but we think, *Hey, it's easier to ask forgiveness than permission. I believe in a God of grace. He understands.*

I, too, believe in a God of grace. I, too, believe that He understands. But I also understand that just becoming a Christian doesn't automatically protect us from dangerous deceptions that can destroy us, as we'll see next.

5

Do Not Be Deceived

You have to wonder about some folks. Product manufacturers certainly do; that's why they include warning labels that seem, well, a little obvious. Consider a few actual product warnings for items sold in the United States:

- On a hair dryer: "Do not use while sleeping."
- On a bread pudding box: "Product will be hot after heating."
- On a clothes iron: "Do not iron clothes on body."
- On a night-time sleep aid: "Warning: May cause drowsiness."
- On a package of peanuts: "Warning: Contains nuts."
- On a child's Superman costume: "Wearing of this garment does not enable you to fly."

As silly as the warnings may seem to most of us, manufacturers include them because some folks actually do burn themselves by trying to iron the shirts they have on and they do break arms and legs and necks by imagining that a ten-dollar Halloween costume enables them to soar like a bird.

Would it surprise you to learn that God put warning labels in His instruction manual, the Bible? He does not include such warnings just for something to do; He includes them because some of us actually do the stupid things He warns us against.

Whenever you see a biblical warning, you can be sure that it points out a real danger, a serious hazard to which many believers remain blind.

Recognize the Danger

I'd like to take a look at several warnings the Bible gives about the dangers of marshmallow grace. As you read the following scriptural passages, keep in mind their intended function. Imagine each one appearing on a big sign, written in bold, capital letters on a flashing neon background, with the words **DANGER AHEAD! EXTREME CAUTION REQUIRED!** at the top.

Most of the warnings we're about to discuss begin or end with a similar family of words. Time after time the Bible broadcasts its most crucial warnings using some version of the phrase, "Do not be deceived." Why use these particular words? Simple. The fact is, many Christians *are* deceived by the lies and errors of marshmallow grace. James and John and Paul and other New Testament writers tell their readers not to be deceived or not to be led astray precisely because some believers *are* deceived and *are* led astray. If no real danger of being deceived or led astray existed, they wouldn't sound their warnings.

The very fact that the Bible issues such ominous warnings indicates that some believers tend to step off cliffs or run into walls or sit on heaps of burning coals. In so doing, they seriously injure themselves. Why should you be one of them? Carefully observe the Bible's warning signs, heed them, and then navigate around the serious dangers they point out.

The Natural Results of Sin

[E]ach one is tempted when, by his own evil desire, he is dragged away and enticed. Then, after desire has conceived, it gives birth to sin; and sin, when it is full-grown, gives birth to death. *Don't be deceived,* my dear brothers. (James 1:14–16)

Do not be deceived: God cannot be mocked. A man reaps what he sows. The one who sows to please his sinful nature, from that nature will reap destruction; the one who sows to please the Spirit, from the Spirit will reap eternal life. (Galatians 6:7–8)

We've already seen that, despite what some believers think, sin can never be tamed or made into a pet. Just when you think you have the critter under control, the kitty turns into a ravenous Bengal tiger and rips you limb from limb. It never sheds its wild DNA.

James reminds us that it is the nature of sin to kill. It might not immediately murder the one who tries to play with it, but "when it is full-grown, it gives birth to death." Always.

In this world, animals give birth to animals that look and act like themselves. Birds hatch birds and dogs give birth to dogs. When James says that full-grown sin gives birth to death, he means that death is what sin *does*. Full-grown sin can't give birth to life anymore than a full-grown dog can give birth to an ostrich. Habitual sin always leads to a death of some kind, as much for the Christian as for the non-Christian. Grace does not change the nature of sin. Sin kills. Always.

And don't forget, James is writing here to *Christians,* to "my dear brothers." It seems that some of them were deceived into thinking that grace somehow protected them from the consequences of habitual, consciously-chosen sin. James felt it necessary to remind them that it didn't. Sin kills. That's its nature.

Paul used the image of farming to express the same idea. When you plant seeds of corn, what do you get many weeks later? Corn. When you plant wheat, what eventually sprouts up out of the ground? Wheat. So if you plant dandelions, why should you expect to harvest bananas?

And yet, Paul apparently had run into some Christians who looked forward to bananas when they had planted nothing but dandelions. Even though they knew they were sinning, they thought God's grace would protect them from serious injury. The apostle wanted to set the record straight and remind them that grace, so great as it is, never changes noxious weeds into nutritious crops. If you "plant" sin, he told his Christian friends, you will harvest whole fields of poisonous produce. And according to the apostle, all your efforts will be rewarded with just one thing: "destruction."

Who needs that? Time to heed the flashing warning sign:

> ## Warning!
> *Don't be deceived: Sin always leads to death.*

Whose Body Is It?

> Don't you know that you yourselves are God's temple
> and that God's Spirit lives in you? If anyone destroys
> God's temple, God will destroy him; for God's temple is
> sacred, and you are that temple. *Do not deceive yourselves.*
> (1 Corinthians 3:16–18)

I don't know how many times I've heard it: "Hey, it's my body.
I can do what I want with it." The speakers usually make the statement to defend their choice of illegal drugs or drinking too much
or repeatedly exposing themselves to sexually transmitted diseases
or whatever kind of self-destructive behavior they're into. And they
think that shuts the door on further debate.

While I can understand why non-Christians might say such a
thing, it baffles me when I hear the words come out of a Christian
mouth. How could the Bible make it anymore explicit? Listen to
Paul: "Do you not know that your body is a temple of the Holy Spirit,
who is in you, whom you have received from God? *You are not your
own; you were bought at a price.* Therefore honor God with your body"
(1 Corinthians 6:19–20).

No true Christian "owns" his or her own body. If you're a believer, your body doesn't belong to you but to God. If you insist on
making the argument, "It's my body, I can do what I want with it,"
go ahead—but then you ought to admit that you're no Christian. To
claim that you're a Christian while at the same time insisting that you
can do what you want with "your" body is like someone claiming to
be a gourmet French chef who refuses to touch food. The two things
just don't go together.

When God bought us (and our bodies!) with the blood of Jesus
Christ, shed on the cross, He didn't take a hands-off approach. He
didn't say, "Friend, you can continue to own that body and use it as
you'd like until the resurrection; then I get it." No, He took posses-
sion of your body the moment you said, "Jesus, I need You to be my
Savior." In fact, He took that old tenement of yours and made it into a
temple fit for the personal residence of the Holy Spirit. Because your
body is now a temple for the Spirit, it has become breathtakingly sa-
cred. Therefore God takes *seriously* what you do with it!

A few of the apostle Paul's friends had forgotten this. They had taken some cues from their corrupt culture and had started sleeping around. *Why not?* they apparently thought. *We enjoy it, and we're going to heaven, anyway. What difference does it make what I do with my body, since I'm going to get a resurrected one? And even if it is wrong, God will forgive me.*

Paul needed to remind his fellow believers that it made an enormous difference to God what they did with the bodies He loaned to them. Didn't they realize that God Himself lived inside those bodies? I guess not; someone had deceived them. So the apostle reminded his Christian friends that God considered the matter very serious—so serious that anyone who consciously did anything to damage God's temple would him- or herself be "destroyed."

Could He *get* anymore serious?

Warning!
Don't be deceived: Your body does not belong to you.

Don't Live for What Killed Christ

Dear children, *do not let anyone lead you astray.* He who does what is right is righteous, just as he is righteous. He who does what is sinful is of the devil, because the devil has been sinning from the beginning. The reason the Son of God appeared was to destroy the devil's work. No one who is born of God will continue to sin, because God's seed remains in him; he cannot go on sinning, because he has been born of God. This is how we know who the children of God are and who the children of the devil are: Anyone who does not do what is right is not a child of God; nor is anyone who does not love his brother. (1 John 3:7–10)

Sometimes the Bible talks so straight that it worries you. You can't possibly misunderstand its meaning, but what it says triggers all kinds of questions. Many passages in the book of 1 John fit this profile.

John has no problem shooting straight. One of his favorite words seems to be "liar," as in, "If anyone says, 'I love God,' yet hates his brother, he is a liar" (4:20). He doesn't leave any question where he stands; he leaves little room for interpretation.

Sometimes all this straight shooting worries us, not only because it seems overly harsh but also because it doesn't seem to square with our experience. John makes a big deal in his letter, for example, over how Christians ought to behave. Repeatedly he says things like, "No one who is born of God will continue to sin" and "Anyone who does not do what is right is not a child of God" and "No one who lives in him keeps on sinning" (3:6). Yet we all know that every human being, with the lone exception of Jesus Christ, has sinned and does sin. So our questions come tumbling out:

"What about 'carnal Christians'?"

"Are you saying that Christians never sin?"

"I thought Christ paid for all of my sins on the cross—past, present, and future?"

How do we understand John's message? First, I think we should recognize that John realized that all humans sin, including Christians. In fact, at the beginning of his letter to fellow believers, he wrote, "If we claim [present tense!] to be without sin, we deceive ourselves and the truth is not in us." And then he explained how we ought to deal with that sin: "If we confess our sins [again, present tense], he is faithful and just and will forgive us our sins and purify us from all unrighteousness" (1 John 1:8–9).

Of course, John knew that genuine Christians sin; that's why he took pains to explain how they should handle it when it happens. Yet throughout his letter, he prefers to focus on the rule not the exception. For John, obedience is the rule; sin is the exception. He can't imagine an authentic Christian who spends most of his or her time sinning. He can't conceive of a real believer who would consciously choose a lifestyle of disobeying God. And so he tells his readers, "Dear children, *do not let anyone lead you astray.* He who does what is right is righteous, just as he [Jesus Christ] is righteous" (1 John 3:7).

John can't fathom that any genuine believer might choose to make sin a habit. Why not? Because sin is exactly what put Christ on the cross. And so he wonders, *How could someone who loves Christ also love the very thing that murdered Christ? It doesn't make any sense.*

John even gives an unexpected reason for why Jesus came to earth. He could have said that Jesus came "to set the captives free" or "to free God's children from their fear of death" or "to give them eternal life." Elsewhere the Bible gives exactly these answers to explain why Christ came. Yet that is not the reason John gives here. He says, "The reason the Son of God appeared was to destroy the devil's work" (1 John 3:8). And what is the devil's work? As it was in the Garden of Eden, as it was in the desert of Jesus' temptation, and as it is in our lives today—the devil's work is always to encourage people to disobey God. Jesus came to destroy that work, so how, John wonders, could any true believer want to join Satan in his work? How could any genuine Christian live for what Christ had to die for?

John answers that he or she couldn't. And all who think they can, he insists, have been led astray.

> # Warning!
> *Don't be deceived: You can't live for what Christ died for.*

Who Inherits the Kingdom?

Do you not know that the wicked will not inherit the kingdom of God? *Do not be deceived:* Neither the sexually immoral nor idolaters nor adulterers nor male prostitutes nor homosexual offenders nor thieves nor the greedy nor drunkards nor slanderers nor swindlers will inherit the kingdom of God. And that is what some of you were. But you were washed, you were sanctified, you were justified in the name of the Lord Jesus Christ and by the Spirit of our God. (1 Corinthians 6:9–11)

For of this you can be sure: No immoral, impure or greedy person—such a man is an idolater—has any inheritance in the kingdom of Christ and of God. *Let no one deceive you* with empty words, for because of such things God's wrath comes on those who are disobedient. Therefore do not be partners with them. (Ephesians 5:5–7)

Many people who believe that the Bible teaches "the eternal security of the believer" (sometimes called, "once saved, always saved"—a doctrine, by the way, that I endorse), nevertheless misunderstand it or misapply it. They reason something like this: *Since I'm saved and nothing can take away my salvation, I'm going to heaven no matter what. Therefore no matter how I sin or how much I sin, I'm safe. I'm "in." So it doesn't really matter how I behave.*

But somebody who truly "gets" grace (not its marshmallow substitute) wants more than anything else to please God. He or she doesn't ask, "How close can I get to the fire without getting burned?" but "How close can I get to God and feel the warmth of His smile?" On a date, he doesn't ask, "How far can I go?" but "How can I respect and honor this girl?" At a party, she doesn't ask, "How much can I drink without getting drunk?" but "How can I make God proud of me while I'm here?" Such on-fire believers have trained themselves to ask, "What's right with it?" more than "What's wrong with it?"

Paul talked about grace more than any other New Testament writer, but he never taught that a Christian's behavior didn't matter. In the two passages quoted at the beginning of this section, Paul got emphatic about the necessary connection between belief and behavior, faith and lifestyle. He warned two separate groups of Christians that they couldn't live like pagans and still expect to wind up in God's kingdom. Those who suggested that they could, Paul warned, spouted nothing but "empty words."

The apostle emphatically declared that the "disobedient" and the "wicked" would not, could not, inherit the kingdom of Christ and of God. "Do not be deceived," he warned one group; "Let no one deceive you," he told the other: if you live like a pagan, you'll wind up with the pagans.

Warning!
Don't be deceived: Current behavior can signal eternal destiny.

On Top of the Ice

For the past several years my parents have lived in the frigid Iron Range country of northern Minnesota. They know all about subzero temperatures. A few winters ago, officials gleefully announced a record low of 60 below zero only a few miles from Mom and Dad's home.

It gets so cold there and the temperatures remain icy for so long that often during the winter residents get to use a temporary highway. When Bear Island Lake freezes over to a suitable thickness, local residents get out their snowplows and clear a path over the lake, creating a shortcut from one side to the other. Then, so long as it remains cold, cars speed back and forth over a temporary highway of ice.

Occasionally, however, the temperature doesn't dip low enough long enough to create the required conditions for an icy roadway. In that case, no winter boulevard across Bear Island Lake gets made, and officials post signs that warn drivers to stay off the ice.

Not everyone pays attention.

More than one vehicle has plunged through the ice into the frigid waters below because the driver ignored the warnings. Whether these folks disbelieved the warnings, thought they knew better, or decided to take their chances, their vehicles (whether automobile or snowmobile) wound up at the bottom of the lake.

God gives His warnings for a reason. Even if the ice looks thick enough, if He posts a "No Driving Here" sign, you'd best stay off the lake. Why wind up at the bottom, looking up, and only then wish you had taken the warning seriously?

6

Will He Find Faith?

When the Son of Man comes, will he find faith on the earth?

LUKE 18:8

*S*ome questions stop you in your tracks. They force you to sit up and take notice, and maybe, just maybe, nudge you to change the way you live.

Not long ago, two long-time friends of mine were having a serious but difficult conversation. Jim said it felt as if his whole world had fallen apart: one girlfriend after another had dumped him, leaving him feeling empty, alone, and hopeless. Greg listened, tried to make a few suggestions, but quickly realized that most of his words fell on ears made deaf by self-imposed misery. So he decided to change tactics.

"May I ask you a question?" Greg said. His depressed friend nodded, but his glassy eyes seemed vacant and lifeless.

"If you continue to do what you've been doing, what will change in your life?" Greg asked. "And if something did change, *why* would it change?" He paused, then looked directly at Jim and added, "Will we be having this same conversation in another five years?"

Jim stirred, and for the first time in their long conversation, looked up. He

> "Will we be having this same conversation in another five years?"

didn't say anything, but his eyes seemed suddenly less remote and dead. Clearly, the last question had rattled him: *Will we be having this same conversation in another five years?*

55

In the next few weeks, much to Greg's delight, Jim started making some healthy changes. His life didn't transform overnight, but it did slowly begin moving in the right direction—for the first time in a very long while.

So what nudged Jim that way? What got him headed toward a more satisfying future? A big part of the answer: a pointed question, spoken by a caring friend.

A Delightful Shower

One day Jesus' traditional adversaries, the Pharisees, asked Him to announce when God would bring Israel into the worldwide magnificence predicted by many Old Testament prophets. No doubt they wanted to hear Him say that God would soon use Him to overthrow the nation's Roman conquerors—that way, they could accuse Jesus of rebellion and get their hated rulers to execute Him.

But, as always, Jesus caught them off guard: "The kingdom of God does not come with your careful observation, nor will people say, 'Here it is,' or 'There it is,' because the kingdom of God is among* you" (Luke 17:20–21). He meant that with His presence, God's kingdom already had begun to take shape.

Yet Jesus also made clear that this long-promised kingdom had not yet blossomed into full form and wouldn't for some time. To His own disciples He said, "For the Son of Man in his day will be like the lightning, which flashes and lights up the sky from one end to the other." No one could miss the kingdom when it finally came in its fullness; it would be obvious to everyone, just like lightning. Yet that amazing day would have to wait because before it arrived its undisputed king—Jesus—"must suffer many things and be rejected by this generation" (17:24–25). The disciples may have wanted the fullness of the kingdom *now*, but Jesus told them they would have to wait—and so will we.

Nobody likes waiting, however, especially for something that they desperately want. To wait patiently, maybe for a long time, requires a lot of endurance. So that's what Jesus told His followers. They needed to develop great endurance in their faith and much per-

---

* Alternate translation suggested by marginal note

sistence in their prayers until the kingdom arrived in its fullness. Just because they didn't immediately receive what they most wanted didn't mean that God had forgotten them or somehow become less gracious. Just because their prayers for "your kingdom come" (Matthew 6:10) didn't get answered right away, didn't mean that they wouldn't get answered at all.

God always honors all of His promises, even if He takes longer than we'd like. "And will not God bring about justice for his chosen ones, who cry out to him day and night?" Jesus asked. "Will he keep putting them off? I tell you, he will see that they get justice, and quickly" (Luke 18:7–8). In other words, God will establish His kingdom in all its glory at the very earliest time possible. He will not delay one second longer than necessary. And then every good thing He promised will rain down on His followers in a delightful shower far beyond their wildest dreams.

And then Jesus asked a more pointed question: "However, when the Son of Man comes, will he find faith on the earth?"

Of Marshmallows and Endurance

All this waiting, Jesus thought, might make some of His followers uneasy. They might start to wonder if God would *ever* do what He promised. If they didn't get what they wanted, when they wanted it, some might decide that this "faith" stuff just doesn't work. They might even begin to doubt that God existed—or if He did, whether it mattered.

Jesus implied that this problem of doubting disciples would get worse the longer they had to wait. If they didn't get what they wanted, when they wanted it, they would see no reason to stick with their faith. They would have little patience and less endurance. So He asked them whether He would find faith when He returned to earth.

I could be wrong, but it seems to me that marshmallow grace leads to exactly this sort of endurance deficit. Real grace enables us to persevere in tough times. A defective understanding of grace doesn't see the need for perseverance, nor does it supply the power for it. When you mistake God's grace for being nice, and when despite your prayers you don't quickly get what you want, what often happens? You tend to respond something like this: *Hey, I didn't sign up for this.*

I thought God was supposed to love me. If He really loved me, wouldn't He give me what I asked for? What use is praying if it doesn't work? I'm out of here.

Could it be that by the time Jesus returns many people in His church will have totally bought the lies of marshmallow grace? Could it be that they will have grown so addicted to "I want it *now*" that they will interpret any delays to answered prayer as proof either that God doesn't exist or that He doesn't really love them? Could it be that the answer to Jesus' question is, "He will find faith—but not much of it"?

More to the point: if Jesus were to return today, would He find real faith in *you?*

The Falling Away

Although the Bible tells us about the return of Christ to encourage us and give us hope, in our day we've managed to make it into a doctrine that deeply divides. Will Jesus come back before, during, or after the Tribulation? Will He rule over a physical, earthly kingdom, or does He intend to reign in every human heart? And on it goes.

While I don't want to add fuel to this fire, I do want to call attention to a comment the apostle Paul made in a letter soaked with encouragement about the second coming of Christ. He seemed to indicate that just before the Lord returns to earth, a lot of professing believers will abandon their faith, just as Jesus hinted in Luke 18. "Don't let anyone deceive you in any way," the apostle wrote, "for that day will not come until the rebellion occurs" (2 Thessalonians 2:3).

Most commentators believe that this verse describes a major "falling away" or "apostasy" in the church just prior to Jesus' return. Robert L. Thomas, writing in *The Expositor's Bible Commentary,* represents this majority opinion when he says:

> "The rebellion" represents [the Greek word] *apostasia,* from which the English word *apostasy* comes. This word points to a deliberate abandonment of a former professed position. . . . Conditions will be ripe for people, especially those who call themselves Christians but are not really such, to turn their backs on God. Then their insincerity will demonstrate itself outwardly. This worldwide anti-God

movement will be so universal as to earn for itself a special designation: "*the* apostasy"—i.e., the climax of the increasing apostate tendencies.[1]

A few scholars teach that the word translated "rebellion" actually means "departure" and refers to the event (usually called "the rapture") in which Jesus takes His church out of the world; but if that is so, then in this passage the word functions far differently than it did anywhere else at the time the letter was written. It seems best to stick with the largest stream of commentators through history and consider 2 Thessalonians 2:3 as a prediction of a worldwide "falling away" in the period just before Christ returns.

And in any case, elsewhere Paul writes, "The Spirit clearly says that in later times some will abandon the faith and follow deceiving spirits and things taught by demons" (1 Timothy 4:1). While we always have to look out for deceptive teachings that lead us away from Christ, the problem will grow much worse the closer we get to the Second Coming.

And what will this "abandoning" of faith look like? Let's briefly consider five aspects of it, outlined in various parts of the New Testament, and see how they all might relate to marshmallow grace.

Designer Doctrine

Back in 1998 the now-defunct *LIFE* magazine did a cover story on God. It asked readers, "When you think of God, what do you see?" In the accompanying article, former Catholic Frank McCourt outlined the beliefs of several significant American religious groups and then revealed his own convictions. "I don't confine myself to the faith of my fathers anymore," he wrote. "All the religions are spread before me, a great spiritual smorgasbord, and I'll help myself, thank you."[2]

McCourt felt perfectly free to pick and choose what he would believe and what he would discard. For many people these days, that means grabbing the marshmallows and dumping the steak. It means accepting the love of God and rejecting the wrath of God. It means championing a kind of grace that allows you to do whatever you want, whenever you want, just so long as it doesn't appear to hurt anyone else. So if you want to believe in things like reincarnation or spirit guides or all-powerful chipmunks, go ahead. One belief is as good as another.

The apostle Paul didn't see things quite that way. He deeply believed in grace and in the freedom that it brings, but he also gave two big thumbs down to designer doctrine. "For the time will come," he wrote, "when men will not put up with

> *Do your ears itch? Then find a guru who will say whatever it takes to give you some relief.*

sound doctrine. Instead, to suit their own desires, they will gather around them a great number of teachers to say what their itching ears want to hear. They will turn their ears away from the truth and turn aside to myths" (2 Timothy 4:3–4).

Since marshmallow grace doesn't want to offend anyone, it encourages people to believe whatever they want to believe, regardless of what the Bible actually teaches. Do your ears itch? Then find a guru who will say whatever it takes to give you some relief. And if that means placing your faith in the Great God Alvin the Chipmunk, go for it.

Sneers, Jeers, and Ridicule

As the time draws near for Jesus to come back, the Bible tells us that scoffers will increasingly attempt to shout down the Christian message. Peter wrote, "First of all, you must understand that in the last days scoffers will come, scoffing and following their own evil desires. They will say, 'Where is this "coming" he promised? Ever since our fathers died, everything goes on as it has since the beginning of creation'" (2 Peter 3:3–4).

You can almost hear them mocking.

- "Hey, it's been two thousand years since the guy went away. How long does it take him to get ready for a simple return trip?"
- "You don't really believe such ancient myths, do you? Don't you know that science has disproved everything that Christianity teaches?"
- "I hope that when he comes back, he brings my pet iguana with him. Ralph died a few years ago and I really miss him."

- "How stupid can you be? I trust in me, not in some dead guy. You're a sucker, plain and simple."

When comments like that come flying your way, what do you do? If you've eaten too many packages of marshmallow grace, you don't do anything. You don't say anything—unless you mumble a few words about how "everybody's entitled to their own opinion."

Don't get me wrong. I'm not for anybody attacking their detractors or becoming more obnoxious than the ones doling out the jeers. Marshmallow grace, however, has *no* answer in the face of stinging sarcasm. It clams up, blushes, or, at best, manages an apologetic, "Well, that's what my parents taught me." Contrast that with a robust grace, the kind that honors Jesus not merely as a Good Buddy but as the Ruler of the universe. Notice how Peter connects a powerful view of Jesus with an effective response to sarcasm: "But in your hearts *set apart Christ as Lord.* Always be prepared to give an answer to everyone who asks you to give the reason for the hope that you have. But do this with gentleness and respect, keeping a clear conscience, so that those who speak maliciously against your good behavior in Christ may be ashamed of their slander" (1 Peter 3:15–16).

Yes, the jeers will come. Yes, the slander will increase. Yes, the mocking and the sarcasm and the potshots will multiply, both from peers and from adults in various positions of authority. The only question is, how will you respond? If you fill your mouth with marshmallows, you won't be able to manage a clear response—if you get out any words at all.

Division Makers

Jesus revealed one of His greatest desires for all His followers in a wonderful prayer He offered just before He went to the cross. "Holy Father," He prayed for His disciples, "protect them by the power of your name—the name you gave me—so that they may be one as we are one. . . . I have given them the glory that you gave me, that they may be one as we are one: I in them and you in me. May they be brought to complete unity to let the world know that you sent me and have loved them even as you have loved me" (John 17:11, 22–23).

Do you see this prayer at work in your own circle of Christian friends? Would you say that your group—with all its popular and unpopular kids, all its jocks and nerds, all its members from one group or another—shows "complete unity to let the world know" that God sent Jesus to be the Savior of the world?

Jesus wanted His followers to function as a single body, despite differences in temperaments or backgrounds or personal histories. The apostle Paul caught this desire when he wrote, "in Christ we who are many form one body, and each member belongs to all the others" (Romans 12:5).

Before Jesus returns to earth, however, this unity for which Jesus prayed will come under special attack. "But, dear friends," wrote Jude, "remember what the apostles of our Lord Jesus Christ foretold. They said to you, 'In the last times there will be scoffers who will follow their own ungodly desires.' These are the men who divide you, who follow mere natural instincts and do not have the Spirit" (Jude 17–19).

> One of the oddest things about marshmallow grace is that while it preaches a sugary-sweet kind of love, in practice it often acts in a most unloving way.

Whenever a theological debate turns into an occasion for scoffing, you can be pretty sure that the Spirit of God had little to do with it. Scoffing among supposedly fellow Christians—believers called to serve the same Lord, on the same side, in the same body—naturally leads to angry divisions. I have evangelical friends in a number of theological camps, and I've never quite understood why some of them love to scoff at those who don't share their perspectives.

(Then again, I'm quite sure I've done the same thing. May the Lord forgive me!)

One of the oddest things about marshmallow grace is that while it preaches a sugary-sweet kind of love, in practice it often acts in a most unloving way. True love, genuine love—love that grows out of a rugged and strong understanding of grace—obeys Christ even when it doesn't feel like it. So when God says something like, "Accept one another, then, just as Christ accepted you, in order to bring praise to God" (Romans 15:7), authentic love asks God for the grace to do just that.

Marshmallow love doesn't. Why should it? It doesn't believe that God would ask it to do anything hard or difficult. So while it may not attack those with whom it disagrees, it most certainly will choose to ignore them or dismiss them and treat them as if they don't exist. And so the unity for which Christ prayed slowly dissolves, not unlike . . . well, a soggy marshmallow gumming up your mouth.

Religious but Reprobate

You might think that as Jesus gets ready to join the angelic armies of heaven in a victorious march to earth people would get less and less religious. They'd abandon any form of worship and become increasingly secular. And for some folks, that's exactly what happens. I live in Oregon, where polls consistently identify my neighbors as among the "least churched" of Americans. They avoid church in larger percentages than anywhere else in the United States.

But don't think that makes most of them less religious! Far from it. They just substitute their own brand of belief for what "organized religion" teaches. Only rarely do you find large pockets of atheists. The majority of Oregonians—like the majority of human beings world-wide—can't seem to get religion out of their system.

When the apostle Paul looked through his prophetic telescope and saw "the last days," he called them "terrible" and listed no fewer than eighteen despicable qualities of the people of that time (2 Timothy 3:1–7). Yet he ended his grotesque list with a sort of catch-all description that, quite honestly, seems a little out of sync with the other terms he used. He says these last-days people will have "a form of godliness but [deny] its power." Imagine that! They may be abusive, boastful, proud, unforgiving, treacherous, and all the rest, yet they still cling to their religion. They have no love for God (v. 4), but they adore their empty and powerless "faith." So the apostle advises his readers, "Have nothing to do with them."

Marshmallow grace inevitably gives birth, over time, to a form of godliness that denies its power. If you worship a God who winks at sin and who doesn't much care what you believe, then eventually you grow far more attached to the rituals and rites of religion than you do to the God supposedly behind them. If your God never stretches out His hand in holy power, then all you really have left is hollow formality. But since all humans naturally long for some collection of traditions or rituals, they'll stick with them even when those traditions cease to point them to the real God.

Of course, this is nothing new. Jesus accused His detractors of honoring the Word of God at the very same time that they dishonored the God who gave it. "You diligently study the Scriptures because you think that by them you possess eternal life," He told them. "These are the Scriptures that testify about me, yet you refuse to come to me to have life" (John 5:39–40).

Throughout history certain groups have held to a form of godliness while denying its power. Yet as the time grows near for Jesus to return, this trend will accelerate—and marshmallow grace will do nothing but help it to pick up speed.

Hatred Up, Love Down

Jesus described one of the most serious symptoms of end-times trouble. "At that time," He said, "many will turn away from the faith and will betray and hate each other, and many false prophets will appear and deceive many people. Because of the increase of wickedness, the love of most will grow cold, but he who stands firm to the end will be saved" (Matthew 24:10–13).

"Because of the increase of wickedness"—as demonstrated in part by the graceless conditions we just considered—"the love of most will grow cold." Jesus' sobering words immediately recall His rebuke of the church in Ephesus: "I hold this against you: You have forsaken your first love. Remember the height from which you have fallen!" (Revelation 2:4–5).

Do you love Jesus more today than you did when you first believed? If you have gorged on marshmallow grace, your answer probably depends on whether life has turned out the way you hoped it would. If you've enjoyed relatively smooth sailing, then you can probably say that you love Jesus more than you did when you became a Christian. If, however, you've had to deal with serious sickness or relationship troubles or a difficult family situation or a terrible time in school, you probably can't say that your love for Jesus has grown. Why not? Because He hasn't "delivered." And so you're mad at Him.

But remember what we said about real grace toward the beginning of this chapter? It endures. It perseveres. It hangs on for dear life. As Jesus says, "he who stands firm to the end will be saved." And the only way anyone stands firm to the end is by feasting on the steak of genuine grace, not by nibbling on a puffy-white substitute.

A Home for Faith

You want to know a secret? I know the answer to Jesus' question about whether He'll find faith on earth when He returns. At least, I know it so long as Ake and Kari live on this planet.

Ake and Kari befriended me many years ago when I moved to Oregon, and they remain dear friends. Life hasn't been easy for this couple. Kari has suffered for more than thirty years with a long list of serious ailments, one of which has required multiple back surgeries. A device implanted in her body constantly drips morphine into her spine to dull the constant pain. Ake has remained the physically healthy one throughout their long and happy marriage, but recently he went under the surgeon's knife for prostate cancer.

Yet I never hear either one of them complain. I hear them rejoice in God even through the occasional grimace—and they do this with real joy and never out of some mistaken notion that they dare not admit their pain. They admit their pain, all right, but they can't seem to help expressing their great joy in the God who has allowed them so many wonderful years together. Their lives overflow with genuine grace, and because of that grace, they thrive. If Jesus came back today, I know for a fact that He'd find faith in their house.

But I doubt you'd find a marshmallow anywhere.

> *The only way anyone stands firm to the end is by feasting on the steak of genuine grace, not by nibbling on a puffy-white substitute.*

7

~~~

How to Be a Feeble Christian

*Y*ears ago I was teaching a Sunday school class about cults. To emphasize a point, I played the role of a cult member trying to convince class members of a false doctrine. Just after I started, a missionary home on furlough walked in and sat down. I didn't think anything of it until I noticed her face getting redder and redder and more and more anxious. Finally it dawned on me that she didn't know I was playing a part; she thought I was really teaching a dangerous doctrine. As soon as I explained my unusual tactic, she let out a huge sigh of relief and exclaimed, "Thank God!"

I suppose I should offer a similar explanation now, lest any reader get the wrong idea. What follows is meant to be tongue-in-cheek and humorously satirical—please don't think I want anyone to become a feeble Christian! We have enough of them already; we don't need anymore recruits. OK?

*Recent polls about the lifestyles of American Christians consistently show
little difference between those who identify themselves as "born again"
and those who claim no religion at all. The two groups' spending and en-
tertainment habits, as well as rates of divorce, promiscuity, and substance
abuse, look nearly identical. Behavior that Christians once considered
outrageous and even shocking today provokes barely a yawn.*

*In such a cultural climate, where "Christian" behavior mimics that
of pagans, you will be sure to find a strong tendency toward lowering the
standards. If you can't hit the target at forty yards, move it to two. So,
unfortunately, it really should not surprise us much if one day soon we
encountered a movement touting the merits of . . .*

The Feeble Christian Hall of Fame!

Baseball has its Cooperstown. The NFL enshrines its greats in
Akron. Even history's top evangelists have their place in Wheaton.

So isn't it about time we honored another group, a crowd of folks
who probably resemble us a lot more than do the superstars? I'm talking, of course, about Feeble Christians.

It's time the spotlight shone on *us!*

After all, we're in the majority. And we're not so bad. We
aren't into vile, gross sin; we really are Christians. Some of the
time we even act like it. It's just that we're . . . well, *feeble*. We
count Ecclesiastes 7:16 as our favorite Bible verse: "Do not be
overrighteous, neither be overwise—why destroy yourself?"

We try hard to blend into our culture. We carry our faith loosely,
like you would a sweatshirt on a muggy afternoon (you never know
when the temperature might drop). We resist temptation so long as
it feels convenient, but we never get too energetic about the task. If a
good time beckons, you won't find our faith getting in the way.

Feeble Christians of the world, it's high time we honored the
trailblazers. It's time to recognize those who set the standards com-
fortably at half-staff. It's time to laud our role models, our mentors,
our Feeble Forebears. Therefore I am proud to present—straight from
the Bible—the *Feeble Christian Hall of Fame!*

He Loves to Be First

As we walk past the imitation marble entry-way, our eyes immediately fix on the stunning portrait to our right: the FCHF's first inductee, Diotrephes. We read about him in 3 John 9–10: "I wrote to the church, but Diotrephes, who loves to be first, will have nothing to do with us. So if I come, I will call attention to what he is doing, gossiping maliciously about us. Not satisfied with

Diotrephes

that, he refuses to welcome the brothers. He also stops those who want to do so and puts them out of the church."

You might think it'd be tough for a leader of the church to aspire to Christian feebility. Wrong! Diotrephes demonstrates that neither position nor title can keep anyone out of the FCHF. It's *behavior* that counts. Review his record:

- *He loved to gossip.* He let his tongue boldly go where none had gone before.
- *He despised hospitality.* He made "charity begins at home" his favorite Proverb (it's *got* to be in Scripture though we have yet to find it).
- *He abused his power.* Those who dared to question his authority quickly found themselves on the business end of his boot.

But more than all of these, one thing qualifies Diotrephes for first place in the Feeble Christian Hall of Fame: his unswerving commitment to himself. He loved to be first. *This me-first attitude is the key to Christian feebility.*

Those who consistently seek their own advantage have an assured place in the FCHF. Forget that stuff about being "bought with his own blood,"[1] that "you are not your own,"[2] that you must "consider others better than yourselves."[3] That might fly for superstars like Paul or John or Billy Graham, but you'll never find *them* in the Hall! No, we reserve the Hall for people committed to themselves, above all. And here's the good news: *you* can reserve your spot right now by following Diotrephes's splendid example!

Set Your Heart on Things Below

Demas

As we leave the smirk of Diotrephes, we walk down the imitation granite hallway and come upon number 2 on the FCHF hit parade, there on your left: Demas. For his story, we turn to 2 Timothy 4:9–10: "Do your best to come to me quickly, for Demas, because he loved this world, has deserted me and has gone to Thessalonica."

Do you long for your own statue to grace the Hall? Then take a cue from Demas. He pioneered one of the surest ways to induction: set your heart on things below, where Christ has been dethroned at the right hand of God.[4]

Sound like a tall order? It's not, really. You might "love this present world" by letting concern for your reputation stop you from identifying publicly with Jesus. When a non-Christian friend spots you somewhere with Bible in hand, turn the cover toward your body so no one can recognize it. Or when someone asks point-blank what you think of Christ, mumble something about Him being a great teacher—almost any crowd finds that acceptable.

Others "love the world" by spending way more time in front of the TV playing video games than in getting to know their Savior or by earning a reputation as committed party animals or by snuggling up to that cute babe or to-die-for hunk known for handing out favors. Any such method will work. Something like it certainly worked for Demas!

Alarmingly, however, it almost didn't. As helpful as Demas's example may be, we must sadly note that he unwisely played with fire. What was he *doing* in the company of the apostle Paul? No sane Feeble Christian would get within twenty miles of such an on-fire believer. Start loitering around someone wholeheartedly committed to Jesus, and before you know it you're thinking of Jesus first. You're giving up the cozy comforts of home, forgetting how good it feels to cruise in a hot ride, and treating the popular crowd like you would anyone else.

Brrrrrrr! It gives us chills.

Fortunately, Demas recovered in time. At the last moment, he cast a longing look at the trinkets of the world and judged their short-lived pleasures preferable to any eternal reward. Oh, how close he came to missing the FCHF! Don't you make the same mistake.

A Feeble Double-Play Combo

After wiping the nervous sweat from our brow, we continue our tour and find a special section dedicated to two outstanding pioneers. Their portraits hang in a specially-constructed alcove that allows visitors to gaze at each simultaneously, even though their portraits hang in separate rooms. Here we honor Euodia and Syntyche, two women described in Philippians 4:2: "I plead with Euodia and I plead with Syntyche to agree with each other in the Lord."

Euodia & Syntyche

It's too bad this dueling duo didn't play baseball; what a feeble double-play combo they would've made! I can hear the late Harry Carey describe the action now: "Bottom of the ninth, one out. The count is 3 and 2, infield at double-play depth. Mitchell winds, delivers . . . it's sharply hit to Euodia at second. She steps on the bag for one—but wait! She's not throwing to Syntyche at first! In fact, she won't even *look* at her! Holy cow, they can't seem to agree on how to complete the double play! Too late to catch Smith at the plate! Well, Cubs fans, that's it. Cubbies lose for the twentieth time in a row . . ."

Cooperstown material they weren't—but that's just the point. While Euodia and Syntyche never would have earned baseball's highest honor, they make a *great* addition to the FCHF. What makes this pair so exciting is their modus operandi. The ES technique is so simple, anybody can master it. All you have to do is pick a fight with someone in the church and keep it sizzling. And who can't do that? For example, you could:

- Get in a snit over some little detail—like the choice of band for an outreach event or the color of the youth room—and refuse to compromise.

- Argue about some fine point of Bible doctrine and forever after consider your opponent "spiritually immature." (In the Middle Ages a fine argument concerned how many angels could dance on the head of a pin. Although that controversy died out, it's easy to uncover thousands of fresh, contemporary disputes. Many have found prophecy to be one such mother lode.)

- Dwell on a wrong done to you, whether intentional or not. Keep turning over in your mind the hurt, the embarrassment, the snub. Tell yourself that you will forgive but not forget. Soon you will have created a division worthy of the feeblest of Christians!

The ES technique can work for any Christian, regardless of background or training. No matter how many Bible verses you have memorized, people you have won to Christ, solos you have sung, or Sunday school classes you have taught, the ES technique can work for *you*. Don't forget that Paul described the method's pioneers as "women who have contended at my side in the cause of the gospel . . . whose names are in the book of life." And yet, simply by feuding with each other, they made it into the FCHF.

So can you!

A Believer in Powerless Prayer

Mary

Strolling now toward the west wing of the Hall, we look up and find our fifth inductee, Mary the mother of John Mark. We find her special qualification listed in Acts 12:12–16, which picks up the action after an angel miraculously springs the apostle Peter from prison:

> [Peter] went to the house of Mary the mother of John, also called Mark, where many people had gathered and were praying. Peter knocked at the outer entrance, and a servant girl named Rhoda came to answer the door. When she recognized Peter's voice, she was so overjoyed she ran back without opening it and exclaimed, "Peter is at the door!" "You're out of your mind," they told her. When she kept insisting that it was so, they said, "It must be his angel." But Peter kept on knocking, and when they opened the door and saw him, they were astonished.

How unfortunate that Luke didn't record the names of Mary's associates, for all deserve recognition. Her name, however, must forever represent those who don't really believe in the staggering power of God's intervening grace. Mary's case especially electrifies because she managed her unbelief despite regular religious practice. No doubt she was one of the first to suggest prayer after Peter's arrest. And it was Mary who offered her home as a meeting place where the faithful could direct their petitions to the throne of grace. Certainly she believed in prayer!

She just didn't believe that God would answer it.

If only we could have eavesdropped on that prayer meeting. The lessons we might have learned! Perhaps it went something like this:

"O Lord, we beseech thee, spare our brother Peter from the gaping jaws of the lion! Do not allow him to suffer the fate of James. Hear us, O Lord!"

"Yes, Lord, deliver our brother from prison. Thou who madest the heavens and the earth, look down from Thy throne and have mercy!"

"Amen and amen, O gracious Lord. Loose his bonds and let him go! Free our dear brother from the power of Thine enemies!"

"Hey!! Everybody! Come look! *Peter is free!* I don't know how, but he is knocking at the door!"

"Rhoda! Can't you see we're having a prayer meeting? Show a little respect, would you?"

"But, mistress Mary. Peter really *is* at the door! Your prayers have been answered!"

"Rhoda, Rhoda, Rhoda. Dear, confused Rhoda. Our brother is in prison, and we are in prayer for him. Now sit down and be still."

"But he *is* at the door, I tell you. Why, even now you can . . ."

"Rhoda!! Are you out of your mind? Now be *quiet!*"

"No, no, you must understand. It *is* Peter! He *is* at the door! Come and see!"

"Mary, wait—do you suppose it could be his angel?"

"Ah, yes Archippus, perhaps you are right. It must be his angel."

"No, NO, *NO!!!* It is *not* his angel! Even now he knocks. Have you all lost your minds? What sort of angel *knocks*?!"

Rhoda never will make it into the FCHF. But Mary—and all who follow in her skeptical, grace-denying footsteps—are even now preparing for themselves a certain place in the Hall.

Beware the Would-Be's!

Leaving the pious portrait of Mary behind, we arrive finally at the end of the Charter Member wing of the FCHF. But step around to your left and discover a mini-hall dedicated to Feeble Christian would-be's, folks who started out well but somehow failed. We preserve their stories as a warning. Never forget that some have started feebly but wound up as strong, mature Christians. Enter this exhibit at your own risk!

Joseph & Nicodemus

The smiling portraits of Joseph of Arimathea and Nicodemus greet us first. Do not let their smiles fool you! Both seemed destined for the FCHF—Nicodemus coming to Jesus at night so as not to be seen,[5] and Joseph trying to protect his religious status by believing in Christ secretly[6]—but in the end they both fell. Each made strong, public stands for Christ, thus removing any hope of nomination to the FCHF.

Not only did both men give up a timid faith for a more daring kind, but the Gospel of Mark actually says Joseph "went *boldly* to Pilate and asked for Jesus' body."[7] Feeble brethren, beware. It could happen to *you*.

Peer now across the dimly-lit room to see another failed Feeble. John Mark began with the right idea, deserting Paul and Barnabas when the going got tough.[8] The young man even served as the catalyst for an infamous apostolic feud. Such a promising start! But somewhere, somehow, things fell apart. Paul, at the end of his most unfeeble life, wrote these dismal words to his good friend Timothy: "Get Mark and bring him with you, because he is helpful to me in my ministry" (2 Timothy 4:11).

John Mark

Alas! The same youth who once bailed out somehow metamorphosed into a tower of strength. Let John Mark be a lesson to you. He let down his guard and allowed God's grace to sweep him right out of the FCHF.

Our Theme Song!

Brothers and sisters of the Feeble Faith, we must rally ourselves to our great cause. And what better way to do that than to adopt a theme song? To make things easy (no use in expending precious energy), why not adapt an old favorite?

"Onward, Christian Soldiers!" immediately springs to mind. Now, no need to get nervous; we will change the song's alarming lyrics. The original sounds much too energetic, hostile, full of action, short on comfort—entirely inappropriate for feeble Christians. But because so many of us already know the tune and we can't very well rid ourselves of it, let's see if it can be rehabilitated. Here's a stab at it:

> Lay down, feeble Christians! Lounging as to snore,
> With the cross of Jesus far behind once more.
> Christ, our friendly Buddy, leads us to the show;
> stretch out on the sofa; see all troubles go!
>
> (chorus) Lay down, feeble Christians!
> Lounging as to snore,
> With the cross of Jesus
> Far behind once more.
>
> Like a bear in winter, sleeps the church of God;
> Brothers, we are resting, pamp'ring our dear bod;
> We are not in motion, all one yawn are we;
> One in entertainment, one in levity!
>   (chorus)
>
> Lives and souls may perish, sin and error reign,
> But the church of Jesus prostrate will remain;
> Gates of hell will never fear a church so pale;
> We have Christ's own promise, but we'd rather fail.
>   (chorus)

Lay down then, ye people! Join our comfy throng,
Blend with ours your snoring, in the drowsy song;
"Sorry!" "Oops!" and "Pardon!" unto Christ the King;
Such will be the only gifts that we will have to bring!
   (chorus)

With this feeble anthem on our lips, we prepare to exit the great halls of the FCHF. As we do, I leave you with one last thought: please don't consider the term "feeble" a negative thing. Remember that feebleness is simply part of the human condition. It's people like us who keep Christ's body from growing muscle bound.

And so we part. But what's this? An empty picture frame! Say . . . could it be waiting for *your* portrait?

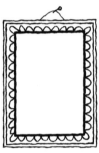

Your Name Here?

PART 2

How Sweet It Is!

8

The Real Deal

A couple of summers ago I got the shock of my year.

My wife and I had traveled back to my hometown for a high school reunion (I won't confess which one), and I looked forward to getting reacquainted with some friends I hadn't seen in a long time. Shortly after we registered, I caught a glimpse of an old buddy I'd known since junior high. "Max" and I used to play basketball together, and he also starred in football.

My mind immediately drifted back to a class we shared as juniors, the only course we ever took together. I don't remember who taught the chef's course, but I do remember some of the dishes we made. For years afterward, I used the recipes and techniques I learned in high school to make éclairs, devil's food cake, and lasagna. I also remember that Max never really did any of the cooking—and especially none of the cleanup—but he always helped himself to substantial portions of the finished product. (Once I do recall him taking a too-heavily floured cake pan, walking over to the window, and dumping clouds of white stuff on several unsuspecting students standing around a couple of floors below, but that could hardly qualify as "clean up.")

While I've forgotten most of what happened in that class, I still vividly remember several conversations we had at the table during the "hands on" part of the hour. While the third member of our group ("Joe") and I worked on following the recipe, Max loved to describe his most recent sexual exploits. He'd go into great detail about whom he'd slept with that week and how race made no difference to him—in bed, he said, things worked pretty much the same with everyone, regardless of skin color.

More than once, Joe would furrow his brow and tell Max that his stories and his behavior disgusted him. Joe was far from a Christian, but he was a senior, so I let him do the talking (in those days I pretty much kept my mouth shut about my Christian beliefs).

Now fast forward to my reunion. There stood Max, hair receding but still trim and muscular. Lisa and I joined him and his wife at their table and started getting caught up. And that's when I got the shock of my year.

> The answer to marshmallow grace is not *jawbreaker grace.*

I discovered that Max not only had become a Christian; he had turned into an *on-fire* Christian. He told me that he helped to pastor a local church, not as a paid minister but as an active layman. Now, of all my friends from high school, I considered Max to be the least likely, by far, to ever take up *any* kind of role behind a pulpit. And yet here he was, telling me how the Lord had changed his life and set him on a different path. He even opened the night's official activities with a very eloquent public prayer.

Max!

How does such an incredible thing happen? What makes it possible? It happens because of the grace of God. It becomes possible when someone—anyone, regardless of background or personal makeup—takes hold of God's grace and lets it turn him or her into someone else entirely.

Change of Direction

What *is* grace, really? How does it differ from its marshmallow counterfeit, and how does it enable on-fire believers to live out their faith in a confident, bold, wildly satisfying, and deeply fulfilling way? Enough of the lie; what's the truth? How can the "real deal" enable us to become not only the people God wants us to be but the people we long to be? And how does it do so without driving us (or those around us) crazy?

I must say one thing up front. The answer to marshmallow grace is *not* jawbreaker grace. You always know when you're talking to someone who promotes jawbreaker grace. It's a counterfeit, too, just in the opposite direction. If marshmallow grace is too soft, jawbreaker grace is too hard. If marshmallow grace leans too much toward the soft and cuddly, jawbreaker grace tilts dangerously toward the cold and prickly. If marshmallow grace says, "So long as it doesn't appear to hurt anybody, it's OK," jawbreaker grace says, "So long as it looks fun and people like it, it's wrong."

Christians who try to live on a diet of jawbreaker grace usually end up compiling long lists of things that they consider "off limits." They talk a lot about holiness and sin and judgment but almost never about joy or peace or mercy. They don't seem to enjoy life much, and they tend to drive everyone around them crazy. (Truth be told, their impossible demands usually drive *them* crazy, too.) It's tough to hang around someone who seems to disapprove of almost everything you say or do.

Real grace, genuine grace, biblical grace—the kind of grace that God extends to you and me—doesn't look a lot like either marshmallow grace or jawbreaker grace. You might say that God's grace takes the best elements of both and excludes the worst traits of each. What else would you expect from a God who "is both kind and severe" (Romans 11:22 NLT)?

Real Grace in Action

If you want to see what real grace looks like, you can't do any better than to observe Jesus Christ in action. If you want to know the nature of divine grace, then look at how Jesus lived, because the "Son reflects God's own glory, and everything about him represents God exactly" (Hebrews 1:3 NLT).

Does that include grace? The apostle John certainly thought so. He tells us that for three years he carefully studied Jesus. After all that time, he ended up calling Jesus "the One and Only, who came from the Father, *full of grace* and truth" (John 1:14). In John's eyes, Jesus not only reflected God's grace; He overflowed with it. And Jesus did so not just some of the time but all of the time. John doesn't mean that sometimes Jesus acted with grace and at other times He spoke with truth. He means that grace and truth filled everything that Jesus did and said, all the time.

The apostle Paul thought the same thing. So he could write to some friends, "For you know the *grace* of our Lord Jesus Christ, that though he was rich, yet for your sakes he became poor, so that you through his poverty might become rich" (2 Corinthians 8:9). That's what divine grace does: it freely and cheerfully dips into its inexhaustible treasure vaults to make desperately poor people filthy rich. And nobody better illustrates God's grace than Jesus Christ.

So how did Jesus act toward the people who crossed His path? How did He express God's grace to the many kinds of men and women, teens and children who bumped into Him? While it's always a little dangerous to generalize, I think we can safely identify three general patterns that often kicked in whenever Jesus dealt with three particular groups. Jesus seemed to react very differently to the people represented in each of these three crowds—but remember, as "the One and Only, *full* of grace and truth," to each group He displayed equal amounts (although not equal expressions) of God's grace. While His responses varied tremendously, the same divine grace lay beneath all.

1. With "sinners" and uninformed unbelievers, Jesus showed tremendous kindness, compassion, patience, and gentleness. He longed for them to experience the love and mercy of God. He made a point to hang out with them, attend their parties, visit their homes, eat and drink with them, walk with them, answer their questions. He did this to such an extent that it offended many of the straight-laced, church-going folks, who sneeringly called Him "a glutton and a drunkard, a friend of tax collectors and 'sinners'" (Luke 7:34).

2. With His own beloved disciples, Jesus could demonstrate considerably less lenience. These followers admitted that Jesus "showed them the full extent of his love" (John 13:1)— and yet He could sharply rebuke them, ask them embarrassing questions, refuse their earnest requests, send them knowingly into difficult and even dangerous situations, give them perplexing instructions, freely express His displeasure at their lack of understanding, and even call one of them "Satan" (Matthew 16:23).

3. With the leading religious leaders and teachers of the day, Jesus could be harsh, blunt, angry, severe, and even violent.

He could call them "snakes" and a "brood of vipers" and ask them, "How will you escape being condemned to hell?" (Matthew 23:33). He had no hesitation about disclosing their secret motivations, no aversion to publicly warning the masses against their teachings, no qualms about violating their most deeply-held traditions. He spoke when they warned Him to keep quiet, and He remained silent when they told Him to speak.

What staggeringly different reactions, wouldn't you say? So how can I claim that Jesus dealt *in grace,* equally, with all three groups? Marshmallow grace likes Jesus' track record with the first group, gets uneasy with what He did with the second, and simply can't fathom what He did with the third. Jawbreaker grace, on the other hand, either ignores or misrepresents Jesus' dealings with the first group, grins at His interactions with the second, and cheers His battles with the third.

> *God's grace motivated Him to take whatever measures—however harsh they might seem—offered the best chance of turning hard hearts into repentant ones.*

But real grace—divine grace—directed and fueled Jesus' response to all three groups. Divine grace flows out of divine love, and perfect love *always* wants the best for those created in God's image. The individuals in the first group saw and felt and experienced the "soft" and "welcoming" side of Jesus because that's what it would take to draw them inside the circle of God's love. The men and women in the second group got either a hand on the shoulder or a kick in the pants, depending on what they most needed at that moment to keep them moving toward a maturing relationship with God. And the stony-hearted religious professionals of the third group felt the wrath and displeasure of Jesus because that's what they most needed—when someone grows desperately ill and near death, only the harshest medicines stand a chance of working. Jesus did not trash the money-changing tables in the temple or call the Pharisees "whitewashed tombs" because He had run out of grace. He did these things because God's grace motivated Him to take whatever measures—however harsh they might seem—offered the best chance of turning hard hearts into repentant ones.

If you want a bad illustration, think of ice cream. I love the stuff and always have. As a kid born and raised in the Dairy State, I gravitated early on more toward ice cream than to cheese (although I still cheer for the Packers, I don't think I could get myself to wear one of those ridiculous cheese hats). At different times I ordered different kinds of ice cream. A lot of vanilla. Some strawberry. Once in awhile cherry. And on special occasions, Blue Moon. Ummm, umm, good. Different flavors but all ice cream.

You could think of God's grace like that. While it comes in different flavors, it's all still grace. So the apostle Peter can write about "God's grace in its various forms" (1 Peter 4:10). Grace comes in different expressions, depending on what the person or situation most needs. But in each case it all gets scooped from the same heavenly carton of grace.

The Worst of Sinners Meets Grace

Ever wonder why the apostle Paul, more than any other New Testament writer, gets identified as "the apostle of grace"? For one thing, of course, he wrote most of the New Testament and spent a lot of his time pushing grace.

But why did Paul so focus on grace? Why did he concentrate so much on it? You might answer, "Because that's what God wanted him to do," and that'd be a pretty good answer. But often God has a way of using something in a person's background or personal history to accomplish what He wants done. I think that could be true in Paul's case.

Paul could never drag his eyes far from the glorious image of grace because he knew he had experienced so much of it. He became like the "certain immoral woman" of Luke 7 who washed Jesus' feet with her tears and dried them with her hair. Jesus forgave the woman's sins and told his offended host, "I tell you, her sins—and they are many—have been forgiven, so she has shown me much love. But a person who is forgiven little shows only little love" (v. 47 NLT).

Paul knew that God had forgiven him of sins far worse than anything the woman had ever done, and so he loved his Lord with a fury that leaves us gasping for air. The great apostle could never forget that once upon a time, not so long before, he had tried to destroy God's church. He had dragged faithful Christians out of their homes and thrown them into prison, then celebrated with shouts of delight when these believers died horribly at the hands of angry mobs hurling sharp rocks. When Paul calls himself "the worst of sinners," he means it. He speaks without a shred of false humility when he writes, "For I am the least of all the apostles, and I am not worthy to be called an apostle after the way I persecuted the church of God" (1 Corinthians 15:9 NLT).

Paul knew better than most that his salvation came about purely through God's grace. He deserved no part of it. That is why he could write, "Even though I was once a blasphemer and a persecutor and a

> *Paul kept on writing about grace because he kept on living grace.*

violent man, I was shown mercy because I acted in ignorance and unbelief. The grace of our Lord was poured out on me abundantly, along with the faith and love that are in Christ Jesus. Here is a trustworthy saying that deserves full acceptance: Christ Jesus came into the world to save sinners—of whom I am the worst. But for that very reason I was shown mercy so that in me, the worst of sinners, Christ Jesus might display his unlimited patience as an example for those who would believe on him and receive eternal life" (1 Timothy 1:13–16). Paul never forgot the awful thing he had done—and how God graciously saved him anyway.

Paul kept on writing about grace because he kept on living grace. He saw himself as a prime illustration of how God's undeserved and unearned kindness not only rescued him from a life of savagery and wickedness, but how it continued to give him the power and the desire to do what pleased God. His idea of grace extended from the past (when he first accepted Christ) to the present (when he drew by faith on the power of Christ to live in a holy way) to the future (when God would exchange his mortal body for an immortal, perfect one). That's why he could sum up his whole gospel message like this: "I preached first to those in Damascus, then in Jerusalem and throughout all Judea, and also to the Gentiles, that all must turn from their sins and turn to God—and prove they have changed by the good things they do" (Acts 26:20 NLT).

Paul knew that he owed his salvation to the grace of God and to nothing else. But he believed equally that the same grace that brought him out of "darkness" and into the "light" also gave him the desire and the power to act in ways that made God, like a proud Father, smile. "For though your hearts were once full of darkness," he told some Christian friends, "now you are full of light from the Lord, and your behavior should show it! For this light within you produces only what is good and right and true" (Ephesians 5:8–9 NLT).

Forget the marshmallows, Paul would say. Throw away the jaw-breakers. Instead, learn to live by the grace that gives you the desire and the power to please God.

What Grace Does

What does grace do for us? Some people honestly believe that the main role of grace is to enable them to resist the temptations that they'd really rather cave in to. But grace does much more than give us the power to stop doing the ugly things that we really want to do.

> *Grace has the divine power to change our desires so that we really want to do what God wants us to do.*

Grace has the divine power to *change our desires* so that we really want to do what God wants us to do. That's why John can say, "This is love for God: to obey his commands. *And his commands are not burdensome*" (1 John 5:3). Not burdensome? What did he mean? John could have said, "This is love for God: to obey his commands. Even if it means gritting our teeth and howling all the way." But he said no such thing. How then could John claim that God's commands are not burdensome? They surely *would* be burdensome and even loathsome to us if they constantly directed us to do things that we hated. But if grace actually changes our desires—if we allow it to do the work for which God designed it—then we can follow David in saying, "I take joy in doing your will, my God" (Psalm 40:8 NLT).

Would you like a test to see if, in your life right now, real grace is operating as God intended? Then answer the following questions: Are your desires showing any signs of changing? Do you find yourself *wanting* to do what God asks you to do in some areas where formerly you either disregarded what He said or you had to grit your teeth and force yourself to obey? If so, then congratulations! Real grace is taking hold in your life, and exciting things lay ahead for you! If not, then recognize that something has gone terribly wrong. You might be chewing on marshmallow grace or gnawing on jawbreaker grace. Why not give them up and opt for The Real Deal?

When The Real Deal operates in your life, things change. You become different from what you used to be. You enjoy life more, not less. You want to do what God asks you to do. Want a few examples? OK. When real grace takes hold in your life, you become . . .

- *More generous*: "With great power the apostles continued to testify to the resurrection of the Lord Jesus, and much grace was upon them all. There were no needy persons among them. For from time to time those who owned lands or houses sold them, brought the money from the sales and put it at the apostles' feet, and it was distributed to anyone as he had need" (Acts 4:33–35).
- *More productive*: "And God is able to make all grace abound to you, so that in all things at all times, having all that you need, you will abound in every good work" (2 Corinthians 9:8).
- *More godly*: God "saved us and called us to a holy life—not because of anything we have done but because of his own purpose and grace" (2 Timothy 1:9).
- *More blessed*: "And now I entrust you to God and the word of his grace—his message that is able to build you up and give you an inheritance with all those he has set apart for himself" (Acts 20:32 NLT).

Marshmallow grace can't give you these things. Neither can jawbreaker grace. But The Real Deal can and will—if you allow it to take root and grow in your life.

Growing in Grace

You want to know one of the best things about The Real Deal? It's like compounding interest on a savings account: it grows over time. As good as it feels right from the start, it gets even better and deeper and richer with age.

When I graduated from high school, my oldest sister, Barb, gave me a Bible. I still use it. Long ago I had to repair its spine with duct tape, and recently I had to plaster the cover in a clear plastic sheet, but somehow it's holding together. At the front of the Bible Barb inscribed a verse in her beautiful, flowing handwriting. I thought about that verse all the way through college, when I got my first job as a newspaper reporter, and all the way to today. I'm glad she chose this verse to personalize her gift. I'd like to leave you with her inscription:

2 Peter 3:18

"But grow in the grace and knowledge of our Lord and Savior Jesus Christ."

9

~mm~

Live Long and Prosper

Why do you call me, "Lord, Lord," and do not do what I say?

LUKE 6:46

I can't remember a time when I didn't like science fiction. I grew up watching shows like *Space Ghost* and *Johnny Quest*. In an old scrapbook I recently discovered an undated certificate that proclaimed me an "official member of the SPACE EXPLORERS CLUB." Along with the certificate I found a letter from a representative of Space Angel himself: "Dear Space Friend, it is my pleasure to award you the enclosed compass ring and welcome you as a member of the SPACE EXPLORERS Club. You will find on the backside of your membership card the Explorers Club code. From time to time, on the program, I'll be sending messages to you in code. I hope you will have lots of fun with it. As a member it's your duty to instruct your friends that both you and I are dedicated to good sportsmanship, clean living, and physical fitness." The signature of Agent G-13 made the letter seem even more impressive.

As I grew older, I remember watching ancient movie shorts of *Flash Gordon* on television and seeing *The Day the Earth Stood Still* at the Boy's Club. I regularly read a comic strip in my *Boys Life* magazine called "Space Conquerors!" And while I sat with Mom at church I used to draw pictures of space ships fighting it out with death rays and enormous jets of fire (not realizing that in the vacuum of oxygenless space, fire would be a pretty hard thing to achieve—even for aliens).

In junior high I got hooked on *Star Trek,* an addiction that continues to this day.

In college I took a science fiction class and wrote a story of my own that I revised a few years later for a literary competition at seminary. My tale featured a disgruntled time traveler who worshiped science and disliked the "faith" aspect of Christianity. He returned to the days of Paul to chemically brainwash the apostle to change the central message of salvation by grace through faith. In the altered days that followed, Hebrews 11:1 came out like this: "Now religion is the substance of things quantitatively proved, the evidence of things observed and empirically evaluated in the light of previous research." The time traveler got his wish . . . sort of. Faith did indeed disappear from Christianity—but without it, the world stayed forever mired in the Iron Age.

Certain themes continually pop up in science fiction, whether in books, movies, games, or television shows. One very common theme goes like this: man creates advanced machines; machines rebel and create havoc. You see such a plot line in classic films (*Forbidden Planet*), TV shows (*Battlestar Galactica*), made-for-TV movies (*Colossus: The Forbin Project*), and current films (the latest installment of *Terminator* and *The Matrix* trilogy). Just last night I watched an episode of *Stargate: SG1* in which hordes of such machines, first created as toys, destroyed a planet and then moved out to threaten the rest of the galaxy. In all these cases, mankind creates the machines either to serve him or to keep him company. But something goes terribly wrong; the machines rebel and end up determined to become the equals (or masters) of their human creators. Chaos results.

An Ancient Plot Line

I don't know if any of these stories consciously borrow their basic plot lines from the Bible, but they certainly might. In essence, this describes exactly what happened in the Garden of Eden.

The first few chapters of Genesis explain how God created humankind in His image so that He might share His love with "sentient beings" patterned after Himself. He did not create them as His equals, but to know Him and love Him and serve Him. Yet they rejected this role and sought to become His peers. Thus Eve swallows the tempter's bold lie: "You will become just like God, knowing everything, both good and evil" (Genesis 3:5 NLT). Adam and Eve eat the forbidden fruit because they want to know "good and evil" apart from God; they want to exist independently of Him and make their own rules. And just like in the movies, chaos results.

Christians believe that God moved to repair the chaos when He sent His Son, Jesus Christ, into the world to redeem His creation and restore men and women to a loving relationship with Himself. Yet many Christians don't have the whole story. They so focus on that loving relationship that they forget what kind of loving relationship it is. It is not and never will be a relationship between equals.

> *We will never "grow out of" the need to obey God.*

While we are patterned in many ways after God, we will never *be* God. We will forever remain less than He is. If you don't believe that, then read 1 Corinthians 15:20–28 and get your world rocked.

Here's the truth: God is still after today what He was after in the Garden. Way back then He wanted men and women, created in His likeness, who would freely, willingly, and gladly love and obey Him within a dependent relationship. He wants exactly the same thing from you and me.

We will never "grow out of" the need to obey God. God will always remain God and we will always remain His creation. Grace does not "free" us from the obligation to obey God; on the contrary, it gives us the power and the ability to both desire and to do God's will. Grace never substitutes our will for God's will. It enables us to achieve God's original design for us: to develop a loving, dependent relationship with Him. Obedience is as much a part of God's design for us today as it always has been. Let's take a quick tour through the Bible to highlight the permanent place of what Paul the apostle called "the obedience that comes from faith" (Romans 1:5).

Obedience: God's Always Been after It

From cover to cover, the Bible details the obedience that God desires from His sons and daughters. He expected it from the beginning and He will expect it at the end.

In the Garden of Eden

When God created the very first humans, He gave them tremendous freedom to explore and enjoy the Paradise He had made just for them. He gave them only one prohibition. "You may freely eat any fruit in the garden," He told Adam, "except fruit from the tree of the knowledge of good and evil. If you eat of its fruit, you will surely die" (Genesis 2:16–17 NLT). Adam and his wife disobeyed God's instructions and so brought catastrophe upon their descendants. "Adam's one sin brought condemnation upon everyone," Paul writes. "Because one person disobeyed God, many people became sinners" (Romans 5:18–19 NLT). God wanted obedience; He got disobedience. And we got death.

In the Time of Abraham

The Bible calls Abraham "the man of faith" and frequently uses him as an example for living (Galatians 3:9). Scripture calls Abraham "righteous" because of his faith (Romans 4:3 NLT). And what kind of relationship did God want with righteous Abraham? Genesis 22 tells how "God tested Abraham's faith *and obedience*" by directing him to sacrifice his beloved son, Isaac, on a lonely mountain (v. 1 NLT). When Abraham passed his terrifying test, God told him through an angel, "*Because you have obeyed me* and have not withheld even your beloved son, I swear by my own self that I will bless you richly. I will multiply your descendants into countless millions, like the stars of the sky and the sand on the seashore. They will conquer their enemies, and through your descendants, all the nations of the earth will be blessed—*all because you have obeyed me*" (Genesis 22:16–18 NLT). Faith came first and obedience followed right behind.

In the Time of Moses

Shortly after God brought Israel out of Egyptian slavery, He directed their leader, Moses, to climb Mount Sinai to hear some preliminary instructions. Before God gave Moses the Ten Commandments, He ordered him to tell the people, "'*Now if you will obey me* and keep my covenant, you will be my own special treasure from among all the nations of the earth'" (Exodus 19:5 NLT).

In the Time of the Prophets

Centuries after the age of Moses, this divine insistence on obedience still rang out loud and clear. Isaiah looked sadly on the disobedience of his people and wrote, "The earth suffers for the sins of its people, for they have twisted the instructions of God, violated his laws, and broken his everlasting covenant. Therefore, a curse consumes the earth and its people. They are left desolate, destroyed by fire. Few will be left alive" (Isaiah 24:5–6 NLT). Unrepentant disobedience always brings disaster. It may come sooner or it may come later, but it always comes.

In the Time of John the Baptist

The ministry of John the Baptist signaled a transition from Old Testament days to the era of the New Testament. Before John's birth, an angel told Zechariah, the boy's father, that John would "precede the coming of the Lord, preparing the people for his arrival. He will turn the hearts of the fathers to their children, and *he will change disobedient minds* to accept godly wisdom" (Luke 1:17 NLT). Matthew sums up the grown-up John's message like this: "Turn from your sins and turn to God, because the Kingdom of Heaven is near" (Matthew 3:2 NLT). When some religious phonies came to John for baptism, he shouted, "You brood of snakes! . . . Who warned you to flee God's coming judgment? Prove by the way you live that you have really turned from your sins and turned to God" (Matthew 3:7–8 NLT). Obedience *matters.*

The Teaching of Jesus

Jesus often taught about the need for obedience. He told one of His disciples, "All those who love me will do what I say. . . . Anyone who doesn't love me will not do what I say" (John 14:23–24 NLT). A little later He told His followers, "When you obey me, you remain in my love, just as I obey my Father and remain in his love" (John 15:10 NLT). When an unidentified woman tried to flatter him by shouting, "God bless your mother!" Jesus replied, "But even more blessed are all who hear the word of God and put it into practice" (Luke 11:28 NLT). Jesus' message didn't change even slightly after His resurrection. In what we often call "The Great Commission," Jesus told us to "go and make disciples of all the nations, baptizing them in the name of the

Father and the Son and the Holy Spirit. Teach these new disciples *to obey all the commands I have given you*" (Matthew 28:19–20 NLT).

The Example of Jesus

Jesus did not merely teach obedience; He lived it. Even as the Son of God, He made it clear that He came to earth to obey His heavenly Father, not to indulge His own desires. "I have come down from heaven not to do my will," He said, "but to do the will of him who sent me" (John 6:38). In case anyone missed the point, He later declared, "I do nothing on my own but speak just what the Father has taught me. The one who sent me is with me; he has not left me alone, for I always do what pleases him" (John 8:28–29). Yet it's one thing to make such a claim; it's quite another to live up to it. Did Jesus make good on His words? We find out at the moment He faced His greatest temptation. On the night of His arrest He clearly foresaw His crucifixion—and He dreaded it. In these last hours, He begged God to change the divine plan. He pleaded for a way out. He implored His Father to find another way to redeem humankind. He shrank from the thought of the cross. So three times Jesus prayed passionately that God would spare Him the pain of having to take our filthy sins on His pure and sinless back. "Father, if you are willing, take this cup from me," He cried out. Yet He did not end His prayer there. He continued: "yet not my will, but yours be done" (Luke 22:42). God willed that Jesus go to the cross, and Jesus obeyed. Thank God!

In the Days of the Church

The church flamed into existence on the Day of Pentecost, when the Holy Spirit (whom Jesus had promised to send) arrived and began to live inside every genuine Christian (Acts 2). Upon these believers, God poured out the full measure of His grace. So did they think this gift of grace freed them from the necessity of obeying the Lord? Hardly. In fact, when Peter and the apostles preached to the Jewish high council about Jesus and His resurrection, they declared, "We are witnesses of these things and so is the Holy Spirit, who is given by God *to those who obey him*" (Acts 5:32 NLT). Paul picked up the same message. He begins and ends his great letter to the Romans—the New Testament's most comprehensive statement on grace—with reminders about the crucial place of obedience in every Christian's life. "Through Christ," he writes in the opening lines of his letter, "God has given us the privilege and authority to tell Gentiles everywhere what God has done for them, so that they will believe *and obey him,* bringing glory to his name" (1:5 NLT). Fifteen chapters later, when Paul finally gets ready to sign off after thoroughly explaining his idea of grace and the faith it produces, he writes, "But now as the prophets foretold and as the eternal God has commanded, this message is made known to all Gentiles everywhere, so that they might believe *and obey Christ*" (16:26 NLT).

> *The writer assumes that if a person believes, he or she also obeys.*

We find the same thing in other New Testament books. A striking example occurs in Hebrews 3:18–19. There the author remembers how the people of Moses' day turned their backs on God's commandments and rebelled in the desert. He recalls how God swore that these rebellious ex-slaves would never enter the Promised Land. And then he asks, "And to whom was God speaking when he vowed that they would never enter his place of rest? He was speaking to those who *disobeyed* him" (v. 18 NLT). But then the writer immediately adds, "So we see that they were not allowed to enter his rest because of their *unbelief*" (v. 19 NLT). So—which is it? What was their problem, disobedience or unbelief? The writer answers, "Yes!" Because these people did not believe, they disobeyed. The writer assumes that if a person believes, he or she also obeys. So it comes as no surprise a little later when he writes that Jesus "became the source of eternal salvation for all those *who obey him*" (5:9 NLT).

I could quote Peter ("God the Father chose you long ago, and the Spirit has made you holy. As a result *you have obeyed Jesus Christ* and are cleansed by his blood," 1 Peter 1:2 NLT) or John ("And how can we be sure that we belong to him? By *obeying his commandments,*" 1 John 2:3) or Jude ("some godless people have wormed their way in among you, saying that God's forgiveness allows us to live immoral lives," 1:4 NLT)—but the pattern seems clear. God expects those of us who drink in His grace to "give [our] bodies to God. Let them be a living and holy sacrifice—the kind he will accept. When you think of what he has done for you, is this too much to ask?" (Romans 12:1 NLT).

At the End of Time

Even when history rolls to a close, God expects our happy obedience to roll on. In a passage that many think pictures a fierce persecution toward the end of history, Satan declares war against "all *who keep God's commandments* and confess that they belong to Jesus" (Revelation 12:17 NLT). A couple of chapters later, the writer describes some coming judgments on the wicked. And he says, "Let this encourage God's holy people to endure persecution patiently and remain firm to the end, *obeying his commands* and trusting in Jesus" (14:12 NLT). And just a few verses from the conclusion of his book and the close of the Bible, the writer tells how he felt so overwhelmed by the extraordinary visions he had seen that he fell down to worship the angel who had shown him these wonders. But the angel said, "No, don't worship me. I am a servant of God, just like you and your brothers the prophets, as well as *all who obey what is written in this scroll.* Worship God!" (22:9 NLT). Finally Jesus Himself puts His stamp of approval on this line of thinking: "See, I am coming soon, and my reward is with me, to repay all *according to their deeds*" (22:12 NLT).

> It is always dangerous to ask, "How far can I go and still be OK?"

Obedience *matters.* It doesn't earn you salvation nor does it keep you saved, but the Bible assumes that obedience will follow genuine faith, just like exhaling follows inhaling or the dawn follows night. It can't conceive of one without the other.

While grace and faith and obedience are different things, God designed one to lead to the next. This helps to explain passages like, "without holiness no one will see the Lord" (Hebrews 12:14) and "There will be trouble and calamity for everyone who keeps on sinning . . . . But there will be glory and honor and peace from God for all who do good" (Romans 2:9–10 NLT). The writers don't mean that you can earn or keep your salvation by the good things you do; but they do see a necessary connection between faith (powered by grace) and obedience. The absence of obedience may well indicate the absence of genuine faith.

This is why it is always dangerous to ask, "How far can I go and still be OK?" Scripture never answers such a question because God has no interest in encouraging His kids to act as disgustingly as possible. He doesn't want them to set up camp on the razor edge of a deadly cliff. Rather, He wants them to spread out their tents on wide, stable terrain that can give joy to their hearts and long life to their souls.

An Excellent and Profitable Way

Recently I began discussing this issue with a long-time believer. He quickly grew concerned and blurted out, "But stressing obedience will just lead to legalism!"

I don't think I could disagree more strongly.

If the Bible stresses obedience from cover to cover, and God inspired the Bible, then who am I to tell God that He got it wrong? Please don't forget that the kind of obedience God wants from us comes through *faith* empowered by *grace*. It doesn't come by gritting our teeth and just trying harder. Consider how Paul saw the process:

> At one time we too were foolish, disobedient, deceived and enslaved by all kinds of passions and pleasures. We lived in malice and envy, being hated and hating one another. But when the kindness and love of God our Savior appeared, he saved us, not because of righteous things we had done, but because of his mercy. He saved us through the washing of rebirth and renewal by the Holy Spirit, whom he poured out on us generously through Jesus Christ our Savior, so that, having been justified by his grace, we might become heirs having the hope of eternal life. This is a trustworthy saying. And I want you to stress these things, so that those who have trusted in God may be careful to devote themselves to doing what is good. These things are excellent and profitable for everyone. (Titus 3:3–8)

Don't forget that this apostle of grace once declared, "I am not free from God's law but am under Christ's law" (1 Corinthians 9:21).

By saying this, Paul did not advocate a new kind of bondage or slavery—but he did want his friends to fully experience the freedom that comes when, by grace through faith, they learned to joyfully obey God's will. On the other hand, he certainly did *not* want them to experience the lousy destiny of an unhappy group described by Isaiah:

> Though grace is shown to the wicked,
>
> they do not learn righteousness;
>
> even in a land of uprightness they go on doing evil
>
> and regard not the majesty of the LORD.
>
> (Isaiah 26:10)

While Paul stressed the role of grace in giving us the will and the power to obey, he never pretended that he had "arrived." Far from it! He freely admitted, "I don't mean to say that I have already achieved these things or that I have already reached perfection! But I keep working toward that day when I will finally be all that Christ Jesus saved me for and wants me to be. No, dear brothers and sisters, I am still not all I should be, but I am focusing all my energies on this one thing: Forgetting the past and looking forward to what lies ahead, I strain to reach the end of the race and receive the prize for which God, through Christ Jesus, is calling us up to heaven" (Philippians 3:12–14 NLT).

But the apostle just couldn't leave it there. He longed to encourage his friends in their own lives of faith, so he described his great, personal desire for the rest of us: "I hope all of you who are mature Christians will agree on these things. If you disagree on some point, I believe God will make it plain to you. But we must be sure to obey the truth we have learned already" (vv. 15–16).

When we follow Paul's excellent advice, we will become great candidates to receive the farewell blessing made famous by a favorite science fiction character of mine. Mr. Spock loved to raise his right hand, spread his outstretched fingers into a "V" (two to each side), and intone, "Live long and prosper."

When God speaks the blessing, however, it won't be fiction (science or otherwise).

10

Help for Ado Annie

My wife, Lisa, really ought to have written this chapter. Just this morning, I asked her if she knew of a Broadway song in which (I thought I vaguely remembered) a young girl admits that she has a hard time saying no.

Lisa stared back at me with those beautiful, blue eyes of hers and said simply, "Ado Annie." Then she started softly singing the lyrics to Annie's famous number, "I Cain't Say No." It turns out that Lisa played Ado Annie twice, once in high school and once in college.

Annie is one of the more colorful characters in Rodgers and Hammerstein's musical *Oklahoma!* While she loves Will, a loveable-but-none-too-bright cowboy, she also has trouble turning down the advances of just about any other guy who throws her a line—and it gets easier the less Will sticks around. At the beginning of the production, we learn that Will has just returned from Kansas City, a happening, "big city" place at the beginning of the twentieth century, the chronological setting for *Oklahoma!*

In her signature song, delivered at a local swimming hole, Annie describes her problem. She *knows* she should keep out of "the pit," but just being with a guy makes her "forgit." So, instead of saying, "No," she ends up saying, "Let's go."

It's too bad that nobody ever directed Ado Annie to the little book of Titus in the New Testament. If they had, she mighta found some pahrful food fer thought that coulda hepped her git outta her fix.

When the Temperature Rises

When a friend suggests that you take part in something that smells a little rotten, do you ever have trouble saying no? When the heat gets turned up and you feel the pressure to join the crowd—even though you know you shouldn't—what do you usually do?

If you're like Ado Annie, the word *no* seldom slides past your lips. In the heat of the moment, you say yes—and often regret it afterward.

> *Grace ripples with the strength not only to help us speak the word "no," but actually to give us the desire to say it.*

You want to know a secret? Every one of us has a lot in common with Ado Annie. We come by this trait naturally. Eve said yes to the snake, even though she had her doubts about his shady proposition. Adam said yes to his wife, even though he definitely knew better than to bite into the fruit already scarred by teeth marks. And we, their children, have been saying yes ever since. So how can we ever hope to say no?

Enter grace.

We will never consistently manage to say no at the appropriate times merely by disciplining ourselves or adopting a rigid code of conduct or asking others to "hold us accountable." Things like this may give some help, but they simply lack the power to get at the root of the problem—what Paul would call the "old man," our natural propensity to sin, inherited from Adam and Eve via their original "yes" to Satan.

Grace, however, ushers us into a whole other ballgame. Grace ripples with the strength not only to help us speak the word "no," but actually to give us the desire to say it. Listen to how the apostle Paul explains this potent force in Titus 2:11–14: "For the grace of God that brings salvation has appeared to all men. It teaches us to say 'No' to ungodliness and worldly passions, and to live self-controlled, upright and godly lives in this present age, while we wait for the blessed hope—the glorious appearing of our great God and Savior, Jesus Christ, who gave himself for us to redeem us from all wickedness and to purify for himself a people that are his very own, eager to do what is good."

Did you catch the radical shift in thinking? Paul mentions "self-control" as a weapon against "ungodliness and worldly passions," but he doesn't put it first. It *can't* come first. Grace has to take the lead-off spot. It has to march first in the parade. Grace is the locomotive that pulls all the rest of the cars down the track. It's the primary rocket that blasts the capsule into space, the main meal of the day, the teeth in the saw that turns a block of wood into a piece of art.

But how? *How* does grace teach "us to say 'No' to ungodliness and worldly passions"? Fortunately for us, Paul doesn't leave us hanging.

Grace with a Face

When the apostle writes, "For the grace of God that brings salvation has appeared to all men," his language reveals that he has something specific in mind. He's not thinking of "grace" in an abstract sense. He's not thinking "unmerited favor" or "free and uncoerced blessing" or anything so ivory tower as that. He clearly has a person in mind.

He's thinking of Jesus Christ.

In Greek (the original language of the New Testament), the words translated "has appeared" point to a definite, identifiable event in the past. Paul has in mind a gargantuan historical episode: the life, ministry, death, and resurrection of Jesus. He looks at the entire earthly story of Jesus and calls it "grace."

In grace, Jesus "appeared to all men" in order to bring them "salvation." Jesus extends His grace to everyone, wherever and whomever they might be, and invites them to receive the eternal life that He alone can provide. They don't deserve it, they have not earned it, they cannot pay for it—and yet, because Jesus is "full of grace and truth," He offers them salvation if only they will place their trust in Him.

The story doesn't end there, however. How could it? The grace of Jesus not only saves believers from the penalty and rightful consequences of their sins; it also gives them the power and the desire to avoid the kind of shady conduct that put Jesus on the cross in the first place. When we spend time thinking about Jesus—pondering what He did, meditating on His words, puzzling over His questions, wrestling with His commands—we come into direct contact with divine grace. And it is this grace, Paul says—the grace that Jesus displayed and embodied in His earthly life by obeying and loving God completely—that teaches believers both negative and positive lessons. Let's take a look at both.

First Off, Then On

Suppose you received an invitation to sit in the front row during the taping of your favorite television show. Maybe you had a friend competing on *American Idol* or a family member appearing on *Late Night with David Letterman* or a neighbor starring in an episode of *Everybody Loves Raymond*. You make all the hotel and flight arrangements and arrange for a cab to take you to the studio. But when the big day comes, disaster strikes.

On your way down from your room to catch the taxi, you run into a wasted group of Australian rugby players just returning from a hard night on the town. One of them spills a full cup of beer on you. Another tears a huge hole in your clothes when he stumbles and tries to use you as an emergency crutch. A third vomits the entire contents of his previous night's revelry all over your back. A fourth . . . well, we won't describe what he does.

What do you do now? Do you ignore your appearance (and your odor) and hurry down to the taxi? Or do you find some way, somehow, to get a change of clothes?

I don't know of anyone who would even think about showing up at the studio without first replacing his or her rank wardrobe. You wouldn't want to risk being seen on national television looking like such a train wreck. Your nose couldn't stand the stench. And probably no one at the studio would let you anywhere near the set in such a foul condition.

It seems obvious, doesn't it? Who would think otherwise? And yet in real life, we often continue to wear grubby, rancid clothes day after stinking day.

The apostle Paul says that you and I *have* received an invitation to appear in person before the biggest celebrity of all, Jesus Christ. We've accepted His invitation. Yet we have a big problem: our old wardrobe has to go. It smells worse than fermented vomit, it looks more like ancient rags than the latest fashion, and its gaping holes would allow an Australian rugby team to pass through. We have only one choice: take off the old clothes and put on some new ones.

In Romans 13:12–14, Paul says it like this: "The night is nearly over; the day is almost here. So *let us put aside* [that is, take off] the deeds of darkness and *put on* the armor of light. Let us behave decently, as in the daytime, not in orgies and drunkenness, not in sexual immorality and debauchery, not in dissension and jealousy. Rather, *clothe yourselves* with the Lord Jesus Christ, and do not think about how to gratify the desires of the sinful nature." Paul gets even more explicit in a longer passage in Ephesians:

> So I tell you this, and insist on it in the Lord, that you must no longer live as the Gentiles do, in the futility of their thinking. They are darkened in their understanding and separated from the life of God because of the ignorance that is in them due to the hardening of their hearts. Having lost all sensitivity, they have given themselves over to sensuality so as to indulge in every kind of impurity, with a continual lust for more.

> You, however, did not come to know Christ that way. Surely you heard of him and were taught in him in accordance with the truth that is in Jesus. You were taught, with regard to your former way of life, *to put off your old self,* which is being corrupted by its deceitful desires; to be made new in the attitude of your minds; and to *put on the new self,* created to be like God in true righteousness and holiness. (Ephesians 4:17–24)

In the next several verses the apostle tackles all kinds of issues: lying, anger, theft, cursing, slander, sex, forgiveness, greed, alcohol—you name it. And he reminds his readers that those who claim Jesus as their Savior simply can't wear clothes designed in hell. They reek of smoke and they look like the devil. And they never fit right.

In Titus, Paul teaches the same lesson in a little different way. He says that grace teaches us two things:

1. "to say 'No' to ungodliness and worldly passions" and
2. "to live self-controlled, upright and godly lives in this present age" (2:12).

God wants us to say "no" to the old and say "yes" to the new. One Bible scholar summarizes Paul's teaching like this: "We must live our present lives differently. Negatively, we must decisively abandon the kind of life which is dominated by lack of reverence for God and by mere worldly interests; positively, we must seek to live rightly in relation to ourselves, to others, and to God."[1]

We are to live like this "in this present age," an age that Paul elsewhere calls "evil" (Galatians 1:4) and "dark" (Ephesians 6:12). In an evil world, Christians are to reflect God's goodness and holiness. In a dark world, believers are to "shine like stars in the universe as you hold out the word of life" (Philippians 2:15–16).

> His grace
> not only saves us,
> it purifies and cleanses
> us—if we'll let it.

The grace of Jesus Christ makes this all possible. His grace not only saves us; it purifies and cleanses us—if we'll let it. Paul says in Titus 2:14 that Jesus "gave his life to free us from every kind of sin, to cleanse us, and to make us his very own people, totally committed to doing what is right" (NLT).

I wonder, are you "totally committed to doing what is right"? Do you feel "eager to do what is good"? The word "eager" suggests a change of attitude, a starkly different outlook from what you had before you became a Christian. Does that describe you?

Even before you put your trust in Christ, it's possible that you felt crummy over some crummy things you did. You probably felt guilty over them and felt remorse that you did such rotten things. You might even have told yourself, "I shouldn't do that" or "I have to stop this"—but I doubt very much whether you thought, *I ENTHUSIASTICALLY DESIRE to do only what is right.* A huge difference exists between "ought to" and "have to" on the one hand and "want to" on the other.

So how do you get from "ought to" to "want to"? How does someone become "*eager* to do what is good"? Grace. Pure grace. And grace starts your journey from "ought to" to "want to" by teaching you to say no to defective ways of living and yes to the things that warm God's heart. Your desires start changing when you make the choice, by grace, to "take off" your old, filthy clothes and "put on" your new, classy ones.

A Final Key

You and I really need to ask ourselves a question. Do we honestly *want* to do what is good? Do we genuinely *desire* to please God by the way we live? If the desire is there, God's grace can more than adequately turn our craving into concrete action.

For those who want it, Paul even gives another key for opening the treasure chest of grace and taking hold of its power to change a life. In the middle of his passage to Titus on saying no to sin and yes to God, the apostle speaks excitedly about the return of Christ. The Second Coming energized Paul like almost nothing else. Paul lived every day with the thought that Jesus soon could come back to earth—this time to rule a worldwide kingdom of righteousness.

Do you want to get serious about your Christian faith? Do you want to become known as a believer "eager to do what is good"? Then start reading what the Bible has to say about the return of Jesus. Take time to study what Jesus said about His second coming. You might be surprised to discover how much the Bible talks about this—and you might get an even bigger surprise over how much your study will change you.

John says, "Yes, dear friends, we are already God's children, and we can't even imagine what we will be like when Christ returns. But we do know that when he comes we will be like him, for we will see him as he really is. And all who believe this will keep themselves pure, just as Christ is pure" (1 John 3:2–3 NLT).

Why does thinking about the Second Coming help us to live more effectively and joyously for God? Simple. When we focus on the return of Christ, we can't help but think of Him in His glory. When He came the first time, He came as the Lamb of God; when He comes the second, He will come as the Lion of Judah. Consider John's fiery portrait of our returning King:

> Then I saw heaven opened, and a white horse was standing there. And the one sitting on the horse was named Faithful and True. For he judges fairly and then goes to war. His eyes were bright like flames of fire, and on his head were many crowns. A name was written on him, and only he knew what it meant. He was clothed with a robe dipped in blood,

and his title was the Word of God. The armies of heaven, dressed in pure white linen, followed him on white horses. From his mouth came a sharp sword, and with it he struck down the nations. He ruled them with an iron rod, and he trod the winepress of the fierce wrath of almighty God. On his robe and thigh was written this title: King of kings and Lord of lords. (Revelation 19:11–16 NLT)

When you think of *that* Jesus, how could you not eagerly desire to do what is good? One writer says, "All who have their hope in Jesus . . . will also be committed to keeping themselves from sin. They will put away every defilement; they will aim to be like him in purity and righteousness. . . . Those who claim likeness to him must be conformed to his earthly life, even as they wait for his coming. To live in sin or disobedience to his commands is to abandon any hope in him. It is the pure in heart who will see God."[2] John longs for us to live in the grace of Jesus, "so that when he appears we may be confident and unashamed before him at his coming" (1 John 2:28).

May I ask you a question? If Jesus were to return today, would you feel confident and unashamed? Or if He were to appear in the clouds tonight, would you feel worried and embarrassed? Your choices today determine how you'll feel tomorrow . . . or whenever He returns.

Grace Stays

My wife had an interesting take on the psychological makeup of Ado Annie, the character from *Oklahoma!* that she twice portrayed on stage. "No one can keep her," she declared, "unless he stays with her."

Ado Annie just couldn't say no until her guy said yes. Once Will gave up his wanderin' ways and committed to stickin' close to his woman, Ado Annie lost all desire to say "yep" to any other guy.

Maybe that's the most powerful way that grace teaches us to say no to ungodliness. Grace, in the person of Jesus Christ, has promised never to abandon us.

"Never will I leave you; never will I forsake you," God promises. (Hebrews 13:5)

"And be sure of this," Jesus declares, "I am with you always, even to the end of the age." (Matthew 28:20 NLT)

You never have to worry that He'll leave you for a little excursion to Kansas City. He's not going anywhere. So when Jesus sticks close to you at all times, you don't have to say yes to evil things. When you know that He remains by your side and in your heart, not just for the long haul but forever, it gets a lot easier to say no.

And a lot more fun, too.

11

~mm~

Dump the Marionettes

When I was about fourteen I attended a weeklong Bible camp with a busload of friends from church. I had no idea what to expect because I had never done anything like it before. And I didn't exactly come prepared.

The conference grounds where we stayed sat on the shores of Lake Michigan, about an eight-hour drive from our church. We went in early July, which meant I could have left just about everything behind except bug spray and the lightest sleeping bag I could find. Instead, I brought my brother's arctic-grade bedroll and no insect repellent.

I'll never forget my first night in the cabin; it still ranks as the most miserable 28,800 seconds of my life. The cabin boasted not a single screen on any of its many windows, and when the blazing sun finally dipped below the lake, the temperature inside our living quarters dropped from about 96 degrees to 95—with no change in the 90-plus percent humidity. So while we got almost no relief from the heat and mugginess, after dark the mosquitoes came storming out in waves of buzzing, biting platoons.

Come bedtime, I lay on my heat-retaining bedroll, the sweat trickling down my cheeks. I didn't really notice, though, because I kept busy trying to swat away clouds of tiny vampires. Finally I could take no more of it. *Nothing could be worse than this!* my mind screamed. So I shook off the vicious swarms, completely enclosed myself in the sleeping bag, and instantly felt relief from my blood-sucking attackers.

That lasted about two minutes.

If the sweat had trickled down my face in the open air, it ran in torrents inside that bag. I felt as though I would suffocate. I endured it for as long as I could, but when it seemed like I could go for a swim without leaving my bed, I threw open the bag, thinking, *Nothing could be worse than this!*

Just a few minutes later, the mosquitoes had me lusting once more for the roasting comforts of a hermetically sealed sleeping bag. Again I dove under the covers with the idiotic thought, *Nothing could be worse than this!*

Do you see a pattern developing?

The maddening cycle continued all night long. For eight miserable hours I alternated between a rock and a hard place (although such a location might have brought considerably more relief). I felt as though I had landed in the pages of Dante's *Inferno*.

I don't remember if the next day we hastily located some window screens or if we acquired some potent mosquito repellent, but I never had to suffer through another night quite like that first one. Thereafter, I could concentrate on things other than survival.

While I could now listen in comfort to the speakers who addressed us, nothing they said stuck with me long. I soon forgot everything they presented. To this day, however, I remember a large sign up high near the podium. "Let Go and Let God," it advised.

For years I pondered that sign. *Let go and let God.* It sounded good. So right. So wise. I agreed with its message then, and I still agree with it today—at least, to a degree.

If by this slogan people mean that we need to entrust our entire lives to God and not leave any corner or secret room outside of His control, I'd say, "Great!" But some people mean something else when they quote these words. They think that they should act like spiritual marionettes—dead blocks of wood stuck to the floor, saying nothing and doing nothing unless an irresistible power from above jerks their strings so hard that they have no choice but to stir. When they say, "Let go and let God," they mean that God has the total and sole responsibility of maturing them into people who look like Christ. They take no responsibility themselves.

"Hey, grace means that God does it all," they say. "Salvation is by grace through faith, and there's nothing I can add to it. It's all God's work." They may even quote a verse or two: "Philippians 1:6 says, 'He who began a good work in you will carry it on to completion until the day of Christ Jesus.' So that's why I don't worry about it. 'Let go and let God,' I always say. God will do what He will do. I'll get there eventually."

But is such a blasé attitude about spiritual growth right? Does grace mean that God excuses us from expending any effort in becoming more like Christ? Is growing in grace all of His work and none of our own?

We cannot take a single step toward spiritual maturity without the grace of God empowering us, and yet it is that very grace that calls us to get off our rear ends and get to work.

Not if the Bible means what it says.

The Necessity of Effort

Before we go any further, let me reemphasize that salvation *is* a gift. We can't earn it and we'll never deserve it. We enjoy eternal life because of God's love not because of anything we do. Jesus paid for our sins on the cross—*all* of our sins—and nothing we do, whether before or after our conversion, can add anything to the worth of His sacrifice.

Yet while we can do nothing to make ourselves righteous before God, once He saves us, the Lord *does* expect us to cooperate with Him—to expend effort, maybe even strenuous effort—until "Christ is formed" in us (Galatians 4:19). We cannot take a single step toward spiritual maturity without the grace of God empowering us, and yet it is that very grace that calls us to get off our rear ends and get to work.

"How can you believe," Jesus asked the Pharisees, "if you accept praise from one another, *yet make no effort* to obtain the praise that comes from the only God?" (John 5:44). Salvation is a gift that comes by grace through believing in Christ. But you'll never hear any praise from God without making an effort to get it.

In a passage that confuses some believers, Paul encouraged his friends in Philippi to "work out" their salvation. Listen to his words: "Therefore, my dear friends, as you have always obeyed—not only in my presence, but now much more in my absence—continue to work out your salvation with fear and trembling, for it is God who works in you to will and to act according to his good purpose" (Philippians 2:12–13).

Paul did not mean that his friends could add anything to the salvation Christ already had provided. He meant, as some classic commentators used to say, that they should "work out" what God had "worked in." If these men and women had truly received eternal life from God, in their behavior they should demonstrate a marked family resemblance with their heavenly Father.

One scholar says that joining God's family "initiates believers into a life with obligations, one of which is to obey Jesus our Lord. Hence, working out salvation does not mean 'working for' salvation, but making salvation operational. Justification must be followed by sanctification, by which the new life in Christ is consciously appropriated and demonstrated."[1]

"Working out" your salvation, of course, takes work. It requires effort. It won't "just happen" on its own. Yet even here, God's grace steps in. Paul tells the Philippians that when they choose to obey God in this matter, He will in turn give them the desire and the energy to accomplish what He asks of them. "For God is working in you," he tells them, "giving you the desire to obey him and the power to do what pleases him" (2:13 NLT).

Nevertheless, it is they (and us) who must "work out" the salvation God has graciously given. It is they (and us) who must "do what pleases him." That takes work. That requires effort—sometimes, a lot of it.

Make Every Effort

To stay mired in their spiritual ruts, Casual Christians have to ignore a truckload of biblical instruction on getting serious about their faith. Decaf Disciples must turn away from verse after verse that directs them to stronger stuff. Blasé Believers need to close their eyes to scores of passages designed to shake them fully awake.

We live the entire Christian life by grace through faith—and yet that grace, time and again, calls us to summon all our strength in a sustained effort to move ahead spiritually.

Do you want to remain a baby Christian your whole life? Whether you ever grow up is largely your choice (Hebrews 5:11–13). But if you ever do grow up, realize this: it will take effort. Consider just a few areas of the Christian life that Blasé Believers, Decaf Disciples, and Casual Christians will never fully experience on this earth:

- **Peace and strength**: "Let us therefore *make every effort* to do what leads to peace and to mutual edification" (Romans 14:19).

- **Close relationships**: "*Make every effort* to keep the unity of the Spirit through the bond of peace" (Ephesians 4:3).

- **Intimacy with God**: "*Make every effort* to live in peace with all men and to be holy; without holiness no one will see the Lord" (Hebrews 12:14).

- **Positive attitude about the future**: "We are looking forward to a new heaven and a new earth, the home of righteousness. So then, dear friends, since you are looking forward to this, *make every effort* to be found spotless, blameless and at peace with him" (2 Peter 3:13–14).

- **Full and satisfying life**: ". . . *make every effort* to add to your faith goodness; and to goodness, knowledge; and to knowledge, self-control; and to self-control, perseverance; and to perseverance, godliness; and to godliness, brotherly kindness; and to brotherly kindness, love. For if you possess these qualities in increasing measure, they will keep you from being ineffective and unproductive in your knowledge of our Lord Jesus Christ" (2 Peter 1:5–8).

The last passage deserves special attention. Peter felt so strongly that his Christian friends should "make every effort" to grow up in their faith that he practically insulted anyone who refused. He insisted that the godly character qualities he outlined—traits developed only by putting out substantial effort—*had* to sprout in a believer's life. And if they didn't? What if such a Decaf Disciple chose to keep sipping the bland junk? Peter called such a person "nearsighted and blind" and declared that he had "forgotten that he has been cleansed

from his past sins." Since Peter didn't want such a bleak life for anyone, he added, "Therefore, my brothers, *be all the more eager* to make
your calling and election sure. For if you do these things, you will
never fall, and you will receive a rich welcome into the eternal kingdom of our Lord and Savior Jesus Christ" (2 Peter 1:9–11).

> *If you don't want
> a "rich welcome"
> to heaven, then by
> all means, join the
> Blasé Believers.*

If you don't want a "rich welcome" to
heaven, then by all means, join the Blasé
Believers. If you want to struggle your
whole life with bouts of wondering whether
you'll escape the lake of fire, then go ahead,
stick with Casual Christianity. If you want
to take a painful dive into an empty spiri-
tual pool, then feel free: sip listless lattes with the Decaf Disciples.

But if you want an exciting, fulfilling, satisfying, productive, and
celebrated Christian life, then you have no choice: you have to exert
some effort. And you could do worse than to follow the example of
Paul the apostle.

Working Hard for God

You would think that if grace meant God favored the marionette
approach, someone like the apostle Paul would "get it." Somebody
who knew grace as thoroughly as he did and who preached it as
widely and as passionately as he did surely ought to know its implica-
tions, both backward and forward. If grace meant, "Hey, take it easy,
bro," then certainly Paul would have headed for the recliner.

Trouble is, he didn't. And he named grace as the reason.

"But by the grace of God I am what I am, and his grace to me was
not without effect," he wrote. So did he power down? Kick back? Slide
into a poolside chaise lounge, beverage in hand? Not on your life. He
continues, "No, I worked harder than all of them—yet not I, but the
grace of God that was with me" (1 Corinthians 15:10).

Paul not only worked hard; he claims he "worked harder than all
of them"—that is, harder than Peter. Harder than James. Harder than
the Twelve. Harder than all the other apostles. He names each one, so
we know who he means by "all of them." And what made him work so
hard? Guilt? Duty? Fear? Fame? No way. Three times in one verse he
identifies the mighty power cell that kept him moving: grace!

Paul worked hard for God—but he'd probably say that God worked mightily through him in grace. And what kind of work did Paul do? "I have worked much harder, been in prison more frequently, been flogged more severely, and been exposed to death again and again," he told his Corinthian friends (2 Corinthians 11:23). He liked to use the word "labor" to describe his efforts (Philippians 1:22; 2:16; Colossians 1:29; 2 Thessalonians 3:8; 1 Timothy 4:10; etc.) and compared them to "being poured out like a drink offering on the sacrifice and service coming from your faith" (Philippians 2:17). With the Colossian Christians he used a strong word (*agonizomai*) to picture his work, a word that eventually dropped into the English language as "agony" (Colossians 1:28–2:1). And he told the Thessalonians, "Surely you remember, brothers, our toil and hardship; we worked night and day in order not to be a burden to anyone while we preached the gospel of God to you" (1 Thessalonians 2:9). He told Timothy that he made it his habit to "labor and strive" in his gospel work (1 Timothy 4:10).

Grace didn't make the apostle Paul lazy. It gave him the energy to accomplish an incredible amount of work. And he made it clear that God wants that same grace to have a similar effect on us.

The Call to Effort

Do you like telling your friends, "Good job," when they do well? Paul did. He especially loved to congratulate his friends who, through grace, worked hard in the Lord.

"We continually remember before our God and Father your *work* produced by faith, your *labor* prompted by love, and your *endurance* inspired by hope in our Lord Jesus Christ," he told his friends in Thessalonica. He also asked them "to respect those who *work hard* among you, who are over you in the Lord and who admonish you. Hold them in the highest regard in love because of their *work*" (1 Thessalonians 1:3; 5:12–13).

Paul asked the members of the church at Rome to "Greet Mary, who *worked very hard* for you," and a little later, "Greet Tryphena and Tryphosa, those women who *work hard* in the Lord. Greet my dear friend Persis, another woman who has *worked very hard* in the Lord" (Romans 16:6, 12).

He didn't want merely to congratulate them, however; he wanted them to learn and do by example. In a second letter to his Thessalonian friends he explained that he worked hard in order to provide "a model for you to follow" (2 Thessalonians 3:9). He told the Philippians, "one thing I do: Forgetting what is behind and *straining* toward what is ahead, I *press on* toward the goal to win the prize for which God has called me heavenward in Christ Jesus. All of us who are mature should take such a view of things. And if on some point you think differently, that too God will make clear to you. Only let us live up to what we have already attained. *Join with others in following my example,* brothers, and *take note of those who live according to the pattern* we gave you" (Philippians 3:13–17).

> Paul served a gracious God, and such a God loves to shower His faithful children with unbelievable gifts, even when all they do is what they ought to do!

Paul also directly admonished his fellow believers to expend effort, even great effort, in service to their King. He told the Corinthians, "stand firm. Let nothing move you. Always *give yourselves fully to the work* of the Lord, because you know that your *labor* in the Lord is not in vain" (1 Corinthians 15:58).

Sound tough? Not a lot of fun? Not very appealing? If that's what you think, you miss the point. Paul never instructed his Christian friends to "work out" their salvation merely because they had to or because they ought to or because God would get mad if they didn't. You see, Paul served a *gracious* God, and such a God loves to shower His faithful children with unbelievable gifts, even when all they do is what they ought to do!

The Place of Rewards

In both the Old and New Testaments, God promises to lavish spectacular gifts on every one of His kids who makes a genuine effort to do what He asks. I wish I had space to go into detail on these rewards, but I don't. So let me just whet your appetite; then *you* do the study.

The psalmist gives the general principle as well as anyone: "One thing God has spoken, two things have I heard: that you, O God, are strong, and that you, O Lord, are loving. Surely you will reward each person according to what he has done" (Psalm 62:11–12).[2]

God doesn't give us many hints about the specific nature of these rewards, other than to say they exceed the wildest imagination of the wildest thinker among us. The closest we get goes like this: "No eye has seen, no ear has heard, no mind has conceived what God has prepared for those who love him" (1 Corinthians 2:9). In other words, the rewards waiting for those who love God (and who prove their love for God by the way they live) stagger the cranium.

Get one thing straight: God's reward is all out of proportion to the actual work you do. It's not a wage; you don't earn it. Think of it as something like a raffle ticket. You can't win unless you plunk down the two-dollar entry fee, but if you hold the Grand Prize ticket, you get to take home a brand new Mercedes Benz SL500 Roadster. You can't say that you earned that roadster—believe me, it's worth a lot more than two bucks—but you do get to keep it because you met the qualifications stated up front.

God's outrageous rewards are something like that. We don't really "earn" them; they're worth phenomenally more than what our little efforts could ever buy. But we do qualify for them when we meet the requirements that God sets out beforehand. When we do what He asks, when we cooperate with His grace and expend some real effort to mature in our faith, serve His people and worship Him, then He enters our names in the heavenly raffle. However, *everyone* who officially enters and plays by the rules wins *waaaaaaaaaaaaaay* more than a fancy car that will one day end up in the junkyard.

And don't get the idea that only apostles and missionaries and pastors and "high profile" types who do "big stuff" qualify for these stupendous rewards. Jesus said, "if *anyone* gives *even a cup of cold water* to one of these little ones because he is my disciple, I tell you the truth, he will certainly not lose his reward" (Matthew 10:42). Paul declared that *all* the work we do through faith qualifies: "Serve wholeheartedly, as if you were serving the Lord, not men, because you know that the Lord will reward everyone for *whatever* good he does" (Ephesians 6:7–8).

If you're already serving in some way, keep it up. If you're not, why not get started? John seems to indicate that a lack of grace-powered effort has nasty consequences for the rewards we could have earned. He tells us, "Watch out that you do not lose what you have worked for, but that you may be rewarded fully" (2 John 8).

So don't get stripped of your medals. Don't lose your heavenly loot. If you don't think you've qualified for much in the way of rewards, then get busy. Can you give a cup of cold water to someone for Jesus' sake? I mean, how much effort does *that* take?

And yet, who knows? You might just get a whole constellation for it.

12

A Bit of Bernie in Me

recently heard that my high school basketball coach died. "Beloit coaching legend passes away," announced the *Milwaukee Journal-Sentinel.* "Legendary Beloit coach Barkin dead at 79," said the *Beloit Daily News.* "Beloit will never forget Barkin," predicted a column by a local sports editor.

Bernie Barkin's teams won two state championships and came in second twice during his thirty-six years of coaching. He won almost twice as many games as he lost. His former players, me included, remember him as a strict disciplinarian and a no-nonsense leader. If you threw a behind-the-back pass that he didn't like (and he didn't like many), you quickly found yourself riding the pines.

Gene Van Galder, who coached with Barkin and later took his place, told the *Daily News,* "I think his great contribution was in providing discipline and stability to the team. When you played for him, you had to toe the mark, otherwise you wouldn't be playing. There was no bending. He used to say, 'There's only one way and it's the Barkin way.' He was very opinionated. When you were a student, you were so intimidated you couldn't talk to him. When you were a colleague, you could bounce back, but could never change his mind."[1]

The same discipline that Coach Barkin brought to the basketball court he used in his chemistry classes. He drilled into our heads what he considered the fundamentals of chemistry. Because of him, I don't think I will ever be able to forget Avogadro's Number: 6.023

X 10^{23}, the quantity of molecules in a "mole" of whatever substance you might be using.

I can't say that I really "enjoyed" Bernie's chemistry class, but I did benefit from it. I learned from his lectures and I learned from his labs. I especially appreciated the labs that highlighted the use of catalysts. I found it fascinating that certain substances, placed in contact with other substances, could provoke a lively chemical reaction with-

> *The changes that grace makes possible always result in something new.*

out themselves undergoing a significant change. By their very presence, catalysts enable or speed up a helpful process.

In class, we used catalysts such as silver and platinum and certain kinds of acids. But as I think about it, I believe we had a much more powerful catalyst in the room. Today I see Coach Barkin himself as our greatest catalyst. He didn't change much over the years, but his presence certainly did provoke a lot of learning and a lot of winning. He reminds me that catalysts come in all forms.

The Christian faith, too, has its own superlative catalyst. It provokes all kinds of change, yet it remains the same. We usually call it "grace."

God Likes New Stuff

The changes that grace makes possible always result in something new. Before grace enters the equation, the old reigns supreme. But in its presence, human lives bubble and steam and change into something never seen before. And this delights God's heart.

On one level, this seems remarkable. Why should God like new stuff? After all, He has been around forever. He never changes (Malachi 3:6). His Son, Jesus Christ, "is the same yesterday and today and forever" (Hebrews 13:8). Both Father and Son claim the same divine name, "The Alpha and the Omega, the Beginning and the End" (Revelation 1:8; 21:6; 22:12–13). So you might be excused for thinking that God would delight in *old* stuff.

Yet while God surely does take pleasure in some ancient things (Jeremiah 6:16), He seems to take even more delight in new stuff. Consider just a few of the new things He loves:

- New songs (Psalm 40:3; Revelation 5:9; 14:3)
- New activities (Isaiah 43:19)

- New names (Isaiah 62:2)
- New compassions (Lamentations 3:22–23)
- New covenant (Jeremiah 31:31; Luke 22:20)
- New command (John 13:34)
- New heavens (Isaiah 65:17)
- New earth (2 Peter 3:13)
- New Jerusalem (Revelation 21:2)

> *He has designed grace with transformation in mind.*

God loves new things so much that He even made special arrangements for the temporary storage of His Son's body. John tells us, "At the place where Jesus was crucified, there was a garden, and in the garden a new tomb, in which no one had ever been laid. Because it was the Jewish day of Preparation and since the tomb was nearby, they laid Jesus there" (John 19:41–42).

God *loves* new things. How much? We get a big clue with the last appearance of the word "new" in the Bible. In Revelation 21:5, God says: "I am making *everything* new!"

And you know what? That "everything" includes you and me.

God's Goal for You

Do you ever wonder about God's highest goal for you? What do you think God most wants to see happen in your life?

That you be happy?

That you be successful?

That you have fun?

That you be safe?

That you feel important?

While all these things have their place and God smiles on each one, they pale in comparison to what He *really* wants for you. More than your happiness, more than your success, more than your safety—in fact, more than anything—God wants you to become "like God in true righteousness and holiness" (Ephesians 4:24). That's why He created you in the first place.

God is not content to allow us to stay the same, old "substances" we were before the catalyst of grace came into contact with our lives. He not only desires this change; He insists on it. He has designed grace with transformation in mind. He intends to use it to remake the "old" us into the "new" us. A phenomenal transformation lies at the heart of His plans for us.

Jesus saved you with a particular goal in mind. "Christ loved the church and gave himself up for her to make her holy," explained the apostle Paul, "cleansing her by the washing with water through the word, and to present her to himself as a radiant church, without stain or wrinkle or any other blemish, but holy and blameless" (Ephesians 5:25–27).

Some might roll their eyes and consider this a pretty fun-killing affair, but the Bible doesn't see it like that at all. The biblical reasoning goes something like this: since you and I were created in God's image and designed from the beginning to become like Him in holiness and righteousness, then the closer we get to that goal, the happier we will be. Holiness doesn't kill fun; it makes it fully possible. So Jude can write that God "is able to keep you from falling and to present you before his glorious presence without fault and *with great joy*" (Jude 24).

Yet we have a problem—a big one. In our natural state, inherited from Adam and Eve, we are anything but holy and righteous. Even after we place our faith in Christ and get His holiness and righteousness credited to our account, in practice we still tend to live according to the *unholy* and *unrighteous* pattern we inherited. That needs to change because God's goal for us remains the same. He wants to make possible and speed up the process of our transformation so that our behavior catches up with our heavenly standing. So He uses a catalyst: grace. He intends to use grace to change the old into something new.

This process of transformation doesn't have anything to do with religion but with the power of God changing you and I from the inside out. As Paul writes, "Neither circumcision nor uncircumcision means anything; what counts is a new creation" (Galatians 6:15).

New Hearts, New Life

God loves new stuff. He delights in renewing decayed things and in restoring damaged ones. One of the decayed and damaged things He feels eager to renew and restore is your old heart.

He told the prophet Ezekiel that He planned to do heart surgery on all of His people. "I will give them an undivided heart and put a new spirit in them," He declared. "I will remove from them their heart of stone and give them a heart of flesh. Then they will follow my decrees and be careful to keep my laws. They will be my people, and I will be their God" (Ezekiel 11:19–20).

God didn't save us and give us new hearts just so we could escape hell and make it to heaven. Neither did He give us new hearts so that we could cut down on the amount of sin we commit. Some of us really think that the Christian life is all about trying to sin less. It's not! The catalyst of grace does not so much reduce our appetite for sin as it vastly increases our hunger for God. It changes our behavior by first changing our desires. Grace makes us eager to do what is good, not sorry that we have to give up what we'd really rather do.

> *New hearts, new life. That's what God has in mind for all of us who claim Jesus as our Savior.*

Repeatedly the Bible talks about chucking the old and embracing the new. God has a lot more in mind for you than merely improving your batting average against demonic curve balls. He wants you in a whole different league altogether.

"Therefore, if anyone is in Christ, he is a new creation; the old has gone, the new has come!" Paul exults (2 Corinthians 5:17). So he tells us, "Get rid of the old yeast that you may be a new batch without yeast—as you really are" (1 Corinthians 5:7). He instructs us to "be made new in the attitude of your minds; and to put on the new self" (Ephesians 4:23–24) and again to "put on the new self, which is being renewed in knowledge in the image of its Creator" (Colossians 3:10).

Peter adds his voice to the chorus. He reminds us that God "has given us new birth into a living hope through the resurrection of Jesus Christ from the dead" (1 Peter 1:3). Early in Peter's ministry, a mighty angel pointedly reminded him about what God had commissioned him to do. The angel freed Peter and some other apostles from jail and told them, "Go, stand in the temple courts and tell the people the full message of this new life" (Acts 5:20).

New hearts, new life. That's what God has in mind for all of us who claim Jesus as our Savior.

The Process Takes Time

Want to hear a confession? For many years I've wondered why God didn't do things differently. Why doesn't this transformation take place instantaneously, the moment we ask Jesus to save us? Why don't our desires immediately change as soon as we place our faith in Christ? Why don't we become in practice what we are in God's eyes the instant we submit our lives to Him?

In other words, why does it have to be such a struggle?

While I suspect the answer has something to do with God demonstrating His jaw-dropping worth before the watching eyes of the universe (see Satan's question in Job 1:9; also 1 Corinthians 4:9 and 1 Peter 1:12), I have to admit that I don't really know. I know only one thing: God has designed this transformation to occur through a *process* made possible by grace and played out over time. And we have to cooperate with this process to benefit from it.

Paul had a hard time with many of the young Christians he led to faith. Some of them got off on detours that led them away from the transformation God wanted for them. A few believers in Galatia, for example, started out well in faith but soon got the idea they had to finish under their own power. "My dear children," Paul wrote to them, "for whom I am again in the pains of childbirth *until Christ is formed in you,* how I wish I could be with you now and change my tone, because I am perplexed about you!" (Galatians 4:19–20).

These believers had genuinely placed their faith in Christ. God gave them new hearts and credited all of His Son's righteousness to their account. He made them into new creations and sent His Spirit to live inside their very bodies. Yet the process of transformation abruptly froze when they abandoned a life of grace through faith in favor of self-effort through willpower. Paul said that Christ had not yet been "formed" in them—in other words, they had short-circuited the process designed to make them behave on the outside like the Christ they already had on the inside.

Paul didn't exclude himself from this process. He never imagined that he had already "arrived." He knew very well that he, too, was still in the process of being transformed into Christ's likeness. He hadn't yet become all that God wanted him to be. So he told the Corinthians, "And we, who with unveiled faces all reflect the Lord's glory, *are being transformed* into his likeness with ever-increasing glory, which comes from the Lord, who is the Spirit" (2 Corinthians 3:18). Paul believed that his personal transformation occurred as he spent time in the presence of his Savior—meditating on His words, obeying His commands, praying. In that way, the "glory" of Jesus increasingly reflected itself in Paul's life.

It's almost as though Paul thought of himself as a mirror. As he spent time in the presence of Jesus, the Lord began cleaning away the grime so that Paul could increasingly do what a mirror is designed to do: reflect the person in front of it. The more

> *The more time Paul spent with Jesus, the more his life reflected his Savior.*

time Paul spent with Jesus, the more his life reflected his Savior. And so through this process he saw himself "being transformed."

God wants the same process of transformation to occur within each of us. In the next chapter we'll talk a little more about how to cooperate, but for now it might help to recognize that the process begins with the mind. "Do not conform any longer to the pattern of this world," Paul writes, "but be transformed *by the renewing of your mind.* Then you will be able to test and approve what God's will is—his good, pleasing and perfect will" (Romans 12:2).

Grace targets the mind as the place to begin this transformation. A lot of people make a big mistake when they try to begin with their behavior. They rightfully feel guilty over the rotten things they do, but then they try to resolve the problem by concentrating on their activities. They make long lists of places they shouldn't go, recruit friends to "hold them accountable," berate themselves for mistakes, and spend a lot of time feeling absolutely miserable. They really want to live a "new" life, but they just can't seem to get there.

In a sense, they fail because they duplicate the error of the Galatians. They begin with faith but try to complete the process with self-effort. Grace suggests a much different way. It focuses first on the mind and its habits, enlisting God's wisdom and power to help us replace old patterns with new ones. All along the way, we depend on the resources of Jesus, not on our own. As Paul says, success in transformation "comes from the Lord, who is the Spirit."

A Bit of Bernie in Me

My mind drifts back once more to my former coach and teacher. Bernie Barkin had a tremendous impact on both his students and his players. One of them, Lamont Weaver, as a sophomore guard hit a fifty-five-foot desperation shot at the buzzer to send the state title game into overtime. He hit two free throws in the second overtime to clinch a victory (and an unbeaten season) and give Barkin his first state championship.

Weaver spent a lot of time with Barkin. He watched what he did, what he said, how he reacted to pressure. After Lamont hit "the shot heard 'round the state," he returned to the sidelines to get with his coach. "After that shot, with all the excitement, the biggest thing he was trying to do was calm us down and explain what we had to do in overtime," Weaver said. "He was excited, but he didn't jump or turn any flips. He didn't show a lot of excitement. He was the general."[2]

Weaver studied his coach and considered him a mentor. In time, Lamont took up the coaching profession himself—and in one sense, he took Bernie with him.

"When I became a head coach myself, I still had a bit of Bernie Barkin in me," Weaver declared. "He demanded respect. Bernie was a great coach, he was a great figure, an all-around real individual."[3]

Transformation—that's the name of the game. It begins to occur when you allow the Holy Spirit within you to change you, bit by bit, into the likeness of Jesus Christ. As you do, you'll discover what a great Coach, a great Figure, and what an all-around real Person your Lord really is . . . and how deeply He wants you to walk in His footsteps.

PART 3

The Aroma of Heaven

13

A Superior Life

Some of my earliest and fondest memories concern bread making. I remember staring up at the kitchen table where steaming loaves of golden brown bread or, even better, rows of hot, butter-brushed rolls sat cooling. Their sweet aroma filled the house, and I could hardly wait until Mom gave the OK to slather a piece with peanut butter and jelly (grape, if my luck held).

Bread making has a way of making the whole house smell delicious. You wouldn't want to eat the drapes or chew on the carpet, but the aroma of freshly baked bread wafting through the house almost makes you think you could.

In some ways, this is hard to understand. Just by looking at the ingredients—flour, salt, water, yeast, etc.—you'd never guess the mouth-watering fragrance that eventually rises from the oven. Yet in the hands of someone who knows what she's doing, these independently unsavory ingredients combine into something wonderful.

In the same way that Mom filled our house with the delectable scent of bread, God wants to fill your life with the delicious aroma of grace. He combines a host of unlikely ingredients and bakes them in the oven of life to create the best-smelling stuff your nose ever whiffed. And He wants you to chow down on the grace He cooks up—it's the only way you'll ever grow.

Christ in You

It's one thing to know what grace *is*. It's another to know how to *feed* on it.

In this chapter I hope to briefly suggest how to live by grace and to illustrate what a life of grace looks like. I also want to show what a life of grace leads to—a joyful celebration of God and His world that powerfully attracts others to the same delightful experience.

Before we go any further, however, let's first lay down the central core of living by grace. Nothing else I say will make any sense or have any positive effect unless you first get this piece of the puzzle in place. The whole Christian life depends on it—that's how important it is. Ready? Chew on this for a bit:

Jesus Christ wants to live through you by His Holy Spirit.

Jesus Christ, the Living One who died and rose again, wants to empower you by His grace to do what you can't do on your own. Remember the verse from 1 Corinthians 15:10 that we looked at in chapter 11 ("Dump the Marionettes")? In that verse Paul writes, "But by the grace of God I am what I am, and his grace to me was not without effect. No, I worked harder than all of them—yet not I, but the grace of God that was with me." The apostle claimed that everything worthwhile he accomplished in his remarkable ministry—and he accomplished a lot—he pulled off by relying on God's grace. He tapped into the power, guidance, love, patience, and wisdom of God to achieve what he never could have on his own. In this way he illustrated a saying of Jesus: "whoever lives by the truth comes into the light, so that it may be seen plainly that what he has done has been done through God" (John 3:21).

Everything of worth that Paul accomplished, he accomplished through his savior. That is why he could tell the Romans, "I will not venture to speak of anything except what Christ has accomplished through me in leading the Gentiles to obey God by what I have said and done" (Romans 15:18). While Paul did the saying and doing, it was Christ who accomplished the work through him. And if Paul did something on his own, he didn't want to talk about it.

The apostle got even more explicit in a famous passage from Galatians: "Christ lives in me," he wrote. "The life I live in the body, I live by faith in the Son of God, who loved me and gave himself for me. I do not set aside the grace of God . . ." (2:20–21).

Paul lived because Christ lived in him. Paul worked because Christ worked through him. Paul succeeded because Christ succeeded for him. Moment by moment—not day by day or week by week or month by month—Paul consciously tapped into God's grace and thus allowed Christ to live through him.

We can do the same thing.

> *Everything of worth that Paul accomplished, he accomplished through his savior.*

A Relationship, Not a Formula

Ever wonder why there doesn't seem to be an "A-B-C" formula in Scripture for a successful Christian life? The Bible appears to lack an organized "ten secrets to a life of stunning achievement" or "seven keys to a winning spiritual autobiography"—why? How can God's Word encourage us to pursue a life of faith powered by grace but then leave out the "how-to" section?

Over the years I've heard countless preachers (or writers like me) say things like, "You cannot live the Christian life on your own strength; you have to depend on God's limitless power." But seldom do they suggest *how* to depend on God's resources and not on your own. They just tell you to do it.

But if you don't know how to do it, how can you do it? Which once more brings up the question: why doesn't the Bible seem to give us this kind of how-to?

I think the answer probably has two parts.

First, the Bible doesn't give us a detailed how-to because it expects that we will learn the basics of living by grace through faith from other, more mature believers. God realizes we need mentors more than manuals, instructors more than instructions. By observing godly men and women and interacting with them in a wide array of life circumstances, we begin to see how a life of faith "works."

Of course, there's a down side to this approach. If you're not regularly interacting with mature Christians, then you're up a creek.

You're unlikely to see how a believer uses faith to draw on God's grace in order to mature in Christ. So when you hear the instruction to "depend on God's power and not your own," it will seem like an order to clap when you have no hands.

> *If you're not regularly interacting with mature Christians, then you're up a creek.*

Second, I think the Bible keeps the how-to instruction to a minimum because God doesn't want us depending on a formula but on our Father. In my experience, we Christians are great at telling others, "God doesn't offer us a religion, He offers us a relationship"—but then we proceed as if we have committed ourselves to a religion, not a Redeemer.

Because such an unfortunate tendency already afflicts us, can you imagine how much worse it might get if we had a list of ten steps to follow or twelve secrets to master or fifty-five keys to discover? We could happily march right out to do the religion thing while completely ignoring the relationship thing.

But God wants to walk alongside us. He wants to be there when we face temptation, rejoice with us when we succeed, encourage us when we feel weak, help us up when we fall. *He* is to remain our constant focus, not our problems or even our spiritual growth. That is why real grace concentrates on loving God more, not on sinning less. That is why it asks, "What's right with it?" rather than "What's wrong with it?" Grace focuses our attention on the true God, not on any lesser god.

Because God insists on remaining the center of our attention—and not some canned system of spiritual self-improvement—He may use vastly different means to bring His individual children to maturity in Christ. While certain elements of His varied "program for spiritual maturity" remain constant (prayer, Bible study, fellowship, service, etc.), He treats each of us as individuals and uses a person-specific, custom-designed plan for every one of His kids.

Do you think He brought Peter along the same way that He developed Paul? Did He take Mary on the same path He led Esther? Did Moses get the same instruction that Isaiah received? Of course not. Each individual faced his or her own difficulties and challenges, and God worked with each one on a Person-to-person basis.

He plans to do the same thing with you.

An Adventure, Not a Cruise

Living by grace has a lot more in common with an adventure than a cruise. An adventure features uncertainty, danger, lots of surprises, and the potential of a big payoff, while a cruise offers a set schedule, relative security, the possibility of a few surprises, and a big bill at the end.

My dad and I went on a cruise to the Caribbean a few years ago. We had a great time (other than an unfortunate incident near the end of the trip involving some dentures; but we won't go into that, other than to say that some little fish in Aruba now have their own artificial reef) and enjoyed exploring both our ship and its exotic ports of call. But you probably shouldn't pick a cruise if you crave spontaneity. Cruise ships work on a set schedule: leave port at 5:30 A.M., sail all day, dinner at 6:00 P.M., show at 10:30 P.M., south-of-the-border banquet at midnight. San Juan on Sunday, St. Thomas on Monday, Guadalupe on Tuesday, Granada on Wednesday, Aruba on Friday.

But what happens if you want to stay two days on Granada or have tacos and flan at 7:00 P.M.? You're out of luck. Cruises operate successfully when they stay on schedule. In an adventure, on the other hand, you never know what may happen next.

Years ago when I worked as an editor for a publishing house, I traveled to Argentina for two weeks. My boss wanted me to assess whether we could help support the church there with Christian literature. For fourteen days, I had a real adventure, never knowing what might head my way.

One day I met with the pastor of a church of 250,000 members. Another day I drove a car in bustling downtown Buenos Aires after getting the instructions, "Don't look in the eyes of other drivers; just keep going. If you look in their eyes, they'll never stop and you could get stuck for hours." One night I expected to speak to a crowd of about 500 believers; instead I found a throng of around 15,000 waiting to hear something from the American (but don't get the idea that they came to hear me; I didn't speak until midnight, and by that time they had already been there for five hours and would stay for another six or seven after I finished my thirty-minute talk).

Cruises are relatively safe, of course, but if you crave adventure, you don't mind a little danger; in fact, you probably prefer it. Cruises may give you a few surprises, but generally speaking, you get what you see in the brochure. Adventures, on the other hand, brim with surprises, some great and some scary. But maybe the biggest difference between a cruise and an adventure is what happens at the end of each. When you leave the cruise ship, you reach for your wallet and pay up. When your adventure ends, it just might yield a huge payoff—maybe the discovery of pirate gold or a new species of life-saving plant or a fascinating new friend.

> *When you live the adventure of grace, you never know what might come next.*

When you live the adventure of grace, you never know what might come next. You can't script it because God remains in control, and He doesn't hand out brochures of coming highlights. You might face real danger, you might lose your health—on a trip to India, I got sick with a fever and had to miss a couple of meetings where I was supposed to speak to a group of pastors—but you'll know you're fully *alive.* Grace loves to surprise you with unexpected twists and turns and promises, in the end, to leave you with far more than anything you ever risked. "I consider that our present sufferings are not worth comparing with the glory that will be revealed in us," said Paul (Romans 8:18).

A Guide, Not a Map

Most of us think we'd love it if God dropped a map in our laps, showing us what cutie to date, which college to attend, whom to marry, where to live, what job to take, and which investments to make. He doesn't do that, however. Instead, He gives us a living Guide.

The Holy Spirit guides us and directs our path. Paul declared that the "sons of God"—believers in Christ—are "led by the Spirit" (Romans 8:14). The Spirit may guide us in any number of ways, and He doesn't restrict His guidance to merely "religious" matters. While Jesus drove out demons by the Spirit (Matthew 12:28) and preached by the Spirit (Luke 4:18), He also traveled from city to city by the Spirit (Luke 4:14) and even felt joy through the Spirit (Luke 10:21).

The same pattern repeated itself in the book of Acts. The first disciples constantly depended on the guidance of the Spirit. Both

Philip (8:29) and Peter (10:19) received specific directions that led to the conversion of nonbelievers. The Spirit guided the church of Antioch to designate some of the world's first Christian missionaries (13:2). Somehow God's Spirit led Paul to avoid a certain region (16:7) and urged him at another time to travel to Jerusalem (20:22), even though He also instructed some other believers to warn the apostle about hardships waiting for him in that city (21:4).

The Spirit continues to guide and direct the followers of Jesus today. The Bible urges us to "live by the Spirit" and says, "Since we live by the Spirit, let us keep in step with the Spirit" (Galatians 5:16, 25). In other words, we are to follow the Spirit's leading—and that means that every believer has the capacity to recognize and act on His guidance.

What does His guidance look like? How does one recognize His direction when it comes? How can we distinguish the Spirit's leading from less reliable sources? While those questions deserve their own book, a few simple tips can help enormously.

First, the Spirit often leads through what He already has said in the Bible. He never leads contrary to what He previously revealed in Scripture—so, for example, He will never lead you or any other Christian to get drunk, have sex outside of marriage, marry an unbeliever, take what doesn't belong to you, attack someone of another race, or do anything else He has prohibited in God's Word.

Second, the Spirit commonly likes to lead His people through a congregation rather than through a private, personal hotline to heaven. Most often in the book of Acts, for example, the Spirit gives His most strategic guidance in the presence of groups of believers. When the church sought His direction on a crucial matter of teaching and behavior (Acts 15), the whole body of believers got together, discussed the situation, and at last came to a Spirit-led consensus. So its leaders could say about their decision, "It seemed good to the Holy Spirit and to us . . ." (v. 28).

Beyond that, listening for the Spirit's voice takes practice and observation. Once again, this is where it's crucial to get involved with mature believers. They can help younger Christians to avoid foolish mistakes and dangerous errors. How many believers would spare themselves deep pain and disappointment by listening to the counsel of more mature followers of Christ? Countless believers have hurt themselves and others by rushing ahead with some harebrained action that they claim "God told me to do." The Spirit does lead, and He may lead in unusual ways—but we must never forget that He is forever the Spirit of wisdom, not the Ghost of silliness.

Do you want to know one of the most powerful ways to invite the Spirit's guidance? You ask for it. And then you keep on asking. You say something profound like, "Lord, I don't know what to do here. I need You to guide me. Help!" Sometimes, He lets you know what you ought to do almost immediately. At other times, He makes you wait (perhaps just to see how serious you are about seeking His guidance). So you keep asking. And asking. And asking. You keep inviting Him into the picture until the picture gets clearer.

> *"Lord, I don't know what to do here. I need You to guide me. Help!"*

Grace doesn't give us a roadmap of our future. Instead it gives us a Guide and instructs us to take His hand and go wherever He goes.

A Life, Not a Lifestyle

Too many people these days concentrate on achieving a certain lifestyle when they really want and need a certain kind of life. The two are not the same thing.

God has designed grace to give you a fulfilling life, not necessarily a hip lifestyle. An obsession with lifestyle focuses on appearance; grace concentrates on substance. A preoccupation with lifestyle majors on the temporary and the quickly passing; grace spends its energies on the eternal and the things that last forever. Those who worry too much about lifestyle look at Christianity and see what they might lose, rather than all they stand to gain. Folks consumed by thoughts of lifestyle relish the timid pleasures they hope to sample, while believers who grow in grace discover the delight of ultimate satisfaction.

Remember what Jesus said? "I have come that they may have life," He declared, "and have it to the full" (John 10:10). Jesus did not leave the glories of heaven and take on human flesh in order to give us a fashionable lifestyle. He came to earth and died on a cross to give us "the life that is truly life" (1 Timothy 6:19).

Only grace can give you a superior life. Only grace can give you the power to live your life to the full. Only by asking Jesus to live through you, by faith, will you experience all the wonders God has planned for you. Grace alone can give you all of that—and only you can make the choice to live by grace.

Grace beyond the Grave

Maybe the most amazing thing about living by grace is that its power in us can continue to work even after we're dead.

When you choose to live by grace and feed on God's resources, astonishing things can happen—even if you're not around to see them. Of all the stories I've heard about a man named George Muller

> *Only grace can give you a superior life.*

and his many remarkable answers to prayer, one hits me more than any other. Muller once said, "The great point is never to give up until the answer comes. I have been praying for sixty-three years and eight months for one man's conversion. He is not converted yet, but he will be! How can it be otherwise? There is the unchanging promise of Jehovah, and on that I rest."

Muller never saw the answer to his decades of prayers for his friend—but that doesn't mean they didn't get answered. The man in question came to Muller's funeral and at the service came to faith in Christ. Think of it: living by grace has such power that it can continue to change the world even after you've left.

Why not see for yourself?

14

Gospel Gothic

still remember one of the first times I ever consciously put into practice a Bible lesson I had learned in church. It happened during lunchtime in a restaurant parking lot a block away from Converse Elementary, where during school hours I toiled in Mrs. Carlson's split fifth/sixth grade classroom.

A dozen or so of us decided to hike across the athletic fields to get some burgers at McDonald's. Led by the popular "couple" of Mark and Diane, we all chatted it up for the few minutes it took to reach our destination. Once we arrived, someone noticed a sales promotion then underway: most of the parked cars had bright green Styrofoam balls affixed atop their radio antennas. This observation triggered a suggestion—wouldn't it be fun to steal them? Mark agreed, and soon our little pack of underage offenders began swiping as many of the trophies as possible.

All except for me. I stood there, immobile, as my friends yelled for me to help. I *really* wanted to join them. All the cool kids were happily darting here and there to fill their pockets with contraband, and they wanted me to join the fun. And what would be the harm? It's not like the Styrofoam balls cost their owners anything; McDonald's had boxes of the things in storage.

And still I stood there. I couldn't get out of my head the words of my Sunday school teacher. Stealing, she said—any kind of stealing—displeased God and hurt His loving heart. Christians shouldn't steal.

Oh, but I *wanted* to! Christian or not, I wanted to join my friends. A fierce battle raged inside my preadolescent head—and in a few moments I silently turned around, ignored the laughing calls of my friends, and headed back to school, alone.

I don't remember anything else about that day. I don't remember what my friends said later or how I felt walking back to class. In one way, it wasn't a huge deal at all—so what if I had joined my friends in their petty larceny? I doubt I would have become a hardened criminal. And yet, for me, the incident did become (although I didn't know it at the time) incredibly important.

> *While grace gives us life, it does so partly by helping us to die.*

It set a precedent in my life of consciously choosing God over something else that promised to deliver more than He could. Not that I always lived up to that precedent! Yet today I look back to that event so long ago and recognize that, at that moment, I began to live out the flip side of living by grace: dying by grace.

We need both if we are to enjoy God's best.

A Bit Further

While grace gives us life, it does so partly by helping us to die. This dying process goes a bit further than merely helping us to say no to some sin (see chap. 10). It trains us to see ourselves in a very different way, a way that makes saying no a great deal easier over the long haul.

The apostle Paul describes his own experience with this dying process in 1 Corinthians 15:31. There he says, "I die every day—I mean that, brothers—just as surely as I glory over you in Christ Jesus our Lord." In the surrounding verses he mentions the personal sacrifices he made in order to tell as many people as he could about the Good News of the death and resurrection of Christ. Paul claims that he and his colleagues "endanger ourselves every hour" and that he "fought wild beasts in Ephesus" (vv. 30, 32).

But why would he do such things, he asks, if the gospel were not true? Why would he constantly risk his neck and the necks of his friends if Jesus Christ hadn't really risen from the dead and commissioned him to preach the gospel of grace? He had given up all kinds of privileges and subjected himself to all sorts of dangers and pressures—in other words, he died daily—in order to faithfully serve the One who rescued him from oblivion.

Yet Paul never saw this daily dying as a sacrifice. He never thought he had given up more than he would gain. He never thought he was doing God a favor by living (and dying) as he did. Quite the opposite! In Philippians 3 he describes many of the great privileges he chose to give up, and then says:

> I once thought all these things were so very important, but now I consider them worthless because of what Christ has done. Yes, everything else is worthless when compared with the priceless gain of knowing Christ Jesus my Lord. I have discarded everything else, counting it all as garbage, so that I may have Christ and become one with him. . . . As a result, I can really know Christ and experience the mighty power that raised him from the dead. I can learn what it means to suffer with him, sharing in his death, so that, somehow, I can experience the resurrection from the dead! (Philippians 3:7–11 NLT)

In Paul's mind, this daily dying that enabled him to truly live had several aspects. Let's look at them next.

Crucified: Past Tense

When someone first puts his or her faith in Christ, several incredible things happen. The term "salvation" covers many of these tremendous accomplishments. And one of the accomplishments of salvation is dying.

We all know that Jesus Christ made our salvation possible by dying on the cross for our sins and rising from the grave three days later. Yet this death-by-crucifixion didn't end when Jesus cried out, "Father, into your hands I commit my spirit" (Luke 23:46). When we call upon Jesus to save us, in a spiritual sense we enter into the physical crucifixion that He suffered for us. The apostle Paul put it like this: "For we know that our old self was crucified with him so that the body of sin might be done away with, that we should no longer be slaves to sin—because anyone who has died has been freed from sin" (Romans 6:6–7).

If grace allows the resurrected Christ to live through us today, grace also allows us to die on the cross with Christ back then—that is, the old us that existed before we placed our faith in Jesus. *That* self, with its addiction to sin and its penchant for evil, died with Christ on the cross. And a corpse has no need to fulfill the wishes of its former master.

> *A corpse has no need to fulfill the wishes of its former master.*

This idea loomed large in the mind of the apostle Paul. He thought it so important that he repeated different versions of it in several of his letters. Ponder three of these references as they appear in the powerful little book of Galatians:

- "I have been crucified with Christ and I no longer live, but Christ lives in me" (2:20).
- "Those who belong to Christ Jesus have crucified the sinful nature with its passions and desires" (5:24).
- "May I never boast except in the cross of our Lord Jesus Christ, through which the world has been crucified to me, and I to the world" (6:14).

Do you think it made a difference for the way Paul lived that he so often dwelled on his "death" with Christ at the cross? When temptation came knocking, do you think it might have been easier for him to keep the door closed? A dead man has no need to turn the knob!

This really isn't a morbid practice but a life-giving one. The apostle wanted his Christian buddies to ponder the same mental picture of death that he kept at the forefront of his mind. Why? So they could truly live. "Or don't you know that all of us who were baptized into Christ Jesus were baptized into his death?" he asked his Roman friends. "We were therefore buried with him through baptism into death in order that, just as Christ was raised from the dead through the glory of the Father, we too may live a new life" (Romans 6:3–4).

Only by dying can we live to the full. Yet our "death" doesn't involve a one-time funeral. We have to hold graveside services every day.

Crucify: Present Tense

It might be nice if, once we accepted Christ and died with Him on the cross, our old self would stay dead. But like a zombie from a bad B-movie, it keeps trying to climb out of the coffin. For that reason we have to keep a barrel of spikes around to keep nailing the decrepit thing back to the cross.

Paul warned his friends about what to expect from this undead monstrosity and reminded them of the importance of dealing properly with it. "For if you live according to the sinful nature, you will die," he told them, "but if by the Spirit you put to death the misdeeds of the body, you will live" (Romans 8:13).

And what kind of "misdeeds of the body" did Paul have in mind? He left no doubt in a passage written to some believers in the ancient city of Colosse:

> *This zombie is persistent, and we have to keep slapping it down.*

So put to death the sinful, earthly things lurking within you. Have nothing to do with sexual sin, impurity, lust, and shameful desires. Don't be greedy for the good things of this life, for that is idolatry. God's terrible anger will come upon those who do such things. You used to do them when your life was still part of this world. But now is the time to get rid of anger, rage, malicious behavior, slander, and dirty language. Don't lie to each other, for you have stripped off your old evil nature and all its wicked deeds. In its place you have clothed yourselves with a brand-new nature that is continually being renewed as you learn more and more about Christ, who created this new nature within you. (Colossians 3:5–10 NLT)

The apostle lists ugly sins, hurtful sins, the kind of sins that destroy relationships and create awful strife and terrible pain—in other words, the kind of sins that all of us commit when we fail to "put to death the misdeeds of the body." This zombie is persistent, and we have to keep slapping it down.

Hollywood has had a lot of fun with movies about the undead (*Night of the Living Dead, Return of the Living Dead*—you get the idea), but the undead force that actually lives within our fallen bodies is no laughing matter. It has to be dealt with every day. Yet so long as we call on the power of grace to do the job, we can keep the casket closed.

Dead to Sin, Alive to God

Don't forget that all this concentration on death and crucifixion has *life* as its goal. Gospel Gothic has value only insofar as it leads to Eternal Excitement.

Do you want to experience the kind of exciting life that God has planned for you? If you do, then you first have to train your mind to consider your body dead to sin—dead like a doornail, dead like a corpse, dead like a zombie with its head blown off. Only then will the *real* you emerge to enjoy the full and satisfying life that God wants to give you.

Again, the apostle Paul gives us some helpful guidance. Notice in the following passage how many verbs he uses that imply a rigorous use of your mind. You can't achieve victory over the old you and claim triumph for the new you without first training your mind to think in terms of death and life.

"In the same way," Paul writes, "*count* yourselves dead to sin but alive to God in Christ Jesus. Therefore do not *let* sin reign in your mortal body so that you obey its evil desires. Do not *offer* the parts of your body to sin, as instruments of wickedness, but rather *offer* yourselves to God, as those who have been brought from death to life; and *offer* the parts of your body to him as instruments of righteousness. For sin shall not be your master, because you are not under law, but under grace" (Romans 6:11–14).

It may seem, at times, that training yourself to think along these lines amounts to little more than an unsophisticated method of self-brainwashing. You might even find yourself thinking, *Let's see, I'm crucified with Christ, but I'm not really crucified after all. That's why I have to keep telling myself I'm crucified. That's why I have to keep putting to death my ugly impulses. I'm dead to sin, but sin still has an attraction for me. My old self died with Christ on the cross, yet I have to consciously refuse to let sin run my life. I am alive to God through Christ, yet I have to purposefully choose to offer the parts of my body to God. It's all so hard. And it all seems just a little phony.*

If you ever think anything like that (I have), then think about something else too. Pull something out of an old math class and remember that if you start with a false premise, you'll wind up with a false result. In life, if you start out with a phony philosophy, you'll end up with a damaged or ruined life. If you try to build on error, you can't help but put up a leaning tower of disaster. If you build on sand, when the storms howl and the rains pour, your house collapses and washes out (in little pieces) to sea.

> *It worked in their lives. Why? Because it rests on a solid foundation of truth.*

Yet did such a thing ever happen to the apostle Paul? Did it happen to Luke? Did it happen to Timothy or Silas or to any other of the early disciples who not only heard this teaching but who lived it out? No. It *worked* in their lives. Why? Because it rests on a solid foundation of truth.

I'm learning to put this truth into practice in a very simple way. Whenever I face some kind of temptation or impulse to do what I know displeases God, I start talking to myself. It helps me to say out loud (or at least in my head), "No, I died to that. How can I still live in it?"

I have found that if I talk to myself in this way at the time of the temptation, I am much less likely later on to talk to myself in another, far less attractive way: "Oh, you idiot. How could you do that *again?* Fool! Imbecile! And you call yourself a *Christian?*"

I prefer the first conversation.

You Don't Have to Scream

The death and life battle to draw on God's grace and live in a way that pleases Him and benefits us goes on 24/7.

My wife and I recently purchased a house that has more problems than we knew about at the time of purchase, and I find new opportunities just about every day to put into practice what I've just written. Yesterday when I returned home from the office, the continuing issues of painting, patching holes, leaking dishwashers, and assorted other challenges gave my old self plenty of openings to climb down from the cross and start screaming. I really wanted to scream, even at my good wife.

But you know what? I didn't *have* to scream. Not at the house, and not at my wife. So for the most part, I didn't. If Zombie Steve crawled down from the cross twenty times, the grace of God helped the new Steve nail him back up there about seventeen times—not a perfect mark, but I'm getting better.

When I get home tonight, I'm sure I'll get another opportunity to improve. And you know what? I think I really might. With grace as my coach and supplier of unlimited power bars, there's no reason why my batting average can't continue to climb.

And the same goes for you.

15

Free to Choose

A couple of summers ago I took a friend's three sons camping. Since they'd never done much of it, we chose a fairly easy route. We visited a state park designed for camping, complete with a grassy, level campsite, convenient electrical outlet and modern restroom facilities around the corner.

Before we reached the campgrounds, I took the boys to a grocery store to stock up on provisions for the weekend. I explained the basics of what we needed, then let them choose the specifics. "You mean . . . we get to choose?" they asked. I nodded.

Slowly they wandered away from the cart, looking for suitable food. Still, each time they came back with some item, they looked at me sheepishly and sort of mumbled, "Is . . . ah . . . would this be OK?" "Sure," I'd say, and flip the thing into the cart. Eventually we collected what we needed and took off for our outdoor adventure.

One day, rather than staying at the campsite, we ventured out to see some sights. We climbed a 218-step (I counted) spiral staircase inside a local monument and threw balsam airplanes into the wind from the top of the tower. We visited a little museum. We took a tour of Civil-War-to-World-War-II-era ruins, guided by a volunteer (also of WW II vintage). And then we decided to get some pizza.

Again, I told the boys they could order whatever they wanted. They looked at their menus but remained silent.

After a few minutes, I said, "So, what would you like?"

"What can we have?" they asked.

"I told you—you can choose anything you'd like," I replied.

They looked at each other, unsure what to do. Finally, one of them made a tentative suggestion. Then they all looked at me. "Fine, if that's what you'd all like," I said.

And finally the light dawned. They really *could* order what they wanted. Five minutes later, they reached consensus. And with a little more prodding, they also chose what they wanted to drink.

Ain't freedom wonderful?

Really and Truly *Free!*

I don't want anything I've written to confuse this crucial issue: in Christ, you are really and truly free. You really can choose how you want to live.

Jesus declared, "You will know the truth, and the truth will set you free" (John 8:32), and, "So if the Son sets you free, you will be free indeed" (John 8:36). Since Jesus *is* "the truth" (John 14:6), He means that in Him you can find and enjoy perfect freedom.

> You really can choose how you want to live.

Paul understood this well. That's why he could write, "Now the Lord is the Spirit, and where the Spirit of the Lord is, there is freedom" (2 Corinthians 3:17). He told one group of Christians who seemed headed toward religious slavery, "It is for freedom that Christ has set us free. Stand firm, then, and do not let yourselves be burdened again by a yoke of slavery" (Galatians 5:1).

What does "freedom" mean? It means you're free. It means you can choose how you want to live. You can turn right or left. Go straight ahead or retrace your steps. Live to please God or live to please yourself. Choose godliness or choose goofiness. You're free.

Free!

Free, But . . .

Just a little while ago I almost wrote, "You're free. No ifs, ands, or buts about it." But then I thought better of it. It's true that the grace of God allows you to choose how you want to live, whether you want to obey Him or disobey Him, make Him smile or make Him frown—but a "but" is connected to this freedom.

No, it's not that kind of "but." It's not the kind of but that says, "You're free, *but* you're free only to live within sharply defined borders. You're not free to step outside those borders. You're not free to do whatever you want. You see that fenced-in area over there? You're free to wander anywhere inside there but nowhere outside it. Your freedom ends at the fence."

Honestly, I don't think that's any kind of freedom at all. That's like the old joke about Henry Ford and what he supposedly told prospective buyers for his Model T: "It comes in any color you'd like, so long as you want black."

The "but" I have in mind isn't that kind of "but." It doesn't constrict or reduce the freedom you have in Christ—*but* it warns you against using your freedom in foolish or destructive ways. Yes, as a Christian you remain absolutely free to choose how you will live. *But* if you freely make decisions opposed to God's stated will, you run the risk of running into brick walls and tumbling over cliffs.

Paul said it like this: "You, my brothers, were called to be free. But do not use your freedom to indulge the sinful nature" (Galatians 5:13). You're free, Paul insisted, and you *could* use that freedom to indulge yourself in all kinds of disgusting and idiotic ways. But why? If God has truly captured your heart, you won't ultimately like it. Besides, you could well hurt yourself or others. So why do it?

Peter had his own take on the subject: "Live as free men, but do not use your freedom as a cover-up for evil; live as servants of God" (1 Peter 2:16). Again, you're free. You can live as you want. But why use your good freedom for stupid things? Why not rather use your creativity to dream up new ways of serving God, which ultimately will give you more satisfaction, anyway?

Count how many times Paul uses the word "but" in the following two passages. Why do you think the word keeps popping up?

> "Everything is permissible for me"—but not everything is beneficial. "Everything is permissible for me"—but I will not be mastered by anything. "Food for the stomach and the stomach for food"—but God will destroy them both. The body is not meant for sexual immorality, but for the Lord, and the Lord for the body. By his power God raised the Lord from the dead, and he will raise us also. (1 Corinthians 6:12–14)

"Everything is permissible"—but not everything is beneficial. "Everything is permissible"—but not everything is constructive. Nobody should seek his own good, but the good of others. (1 Corinthians 10:23–24)

He could hardly make it more plain. Yes, you can choose to do things that don't benefit you, do create addictions, will pass out of existence and are not constructive. But why? In the long run such things will only harm you, injure others, and cause you loads of regret. And where is the wisdom in that?

> *We had the freedom to choose as we desired,* **but we did not have the freedom to avoid the consequences** *of our freely-chosen course of action.*

As a senior in high school I went bowling with a friend. Around midnight, on our way home, Curt turned to me from behind the driver's seat and said, "Hey, why don't we make the people behind us think no one is driving the car?" I could have said no. I should have said no. I thought it wise to say no. But I didn't say anything. Hearing no objections, Curt flopped down in the seat and asked me to grab the steering wheel from the passenger's side.

Ha, ha. What a joke. For about fifteen seconds. Suddenly I saw that his dad's brand-new car was careering toward the curb and what lay a short distance beyond it: a telephone pole, a tree, a six-foot hedge, and an iron railing attached to a rather stationary house.

Curt had jammed his knee against the steering wheel and I couldn't budge the thing. When I shouted, "Curt!" he popped up and barely managed to avoid the tree and the telephone pole. We drove through the hedge, knocked down the porch railing, and tore up the lawn. We wound up on the other side of the street, straddling a concrete gas pump stand at an abandoned station. The police showed up a few minutes later, and Curt had some explaining to do. And me? I took a walk down the street—what any coward would do.

Curt had the freedom in that moment to drive as he wanted. I had the freedom to object, agree, or stay silent. We exercised all kinds of freedom that night. Nevertheless, we ran headlong into an immovable "but." We had the freedom to choose as we desired, *but* we did not have the freedom to avoid the consequences of our freely-chosen course of action.

The "Perhaps" of God's Grace

You are free in Christ to do what you choose. You can make either wise or foolish choices—but you are most definitely *not* free to dictate the cost of those choices.

The freedom inherent in grace does not give anyone blanket immunity from the natural penalties of sin. Grace does not invalidate the principle, "you reap what you sow."

Our culture and even many of us in the church have a hard time understanding this. We hear so much about God's love and grace that we feel great surprise and even offense when our foolish choices come back to bite us. We want to blame others.

A few years ago, sports radio talk shows across the country had a field day with a story out of the South. The University of Alabama had named Mike Price as the new head football coach of the Crimson Tide, the school's third coach in the previous four years. The once-ballyhooed program had suffered a series of setbacks and the NCAA placed it on probation, making it ineligible for a postseason bowl game. It needed a coach who could rebuild the school's battered reputation and restore some dignity to the Tide.

Instead, the new head man got fired, even before he could coach his first game. Why? News reports talked about excessive drinking, an embarrassing incident at a strip club, and improper use of a credit card. *Sports Illustrated* reported much more lurid details, but it's not necessary to go into them here.[1] I bring up the story only to note the fired coach's reaction.

"Whatever happened to second chances in life?" Price demanded during a press conference subsequent to his dismissal.[2] He made it clear that he felt like a victim of an overzealous university administration. "I don't think the punishment fits the crime," he said. "I strongly feel that I was the man that could have put this behind us. I think President Witt is making a mistake. He's not breaking the law, but he's making an error in judgment."[3] Price confessed to screwing up, but he felt he had a right to grace. "To the university and entire 'Bama

Nation, I admit making mistakes and at times inappropriate behavior, but I also ask for your forgiveness," Price said.[4]

It seems as though he really meant, "I *demand* your forgiveness."

But grace that is deserved is no grace at all. Grace must be given freely, not out of obligation. Therefore no one can presume upon grace, whether in college athletics or in the Christian life.

> *But grace that is deserved is no grace at all.*

Of course, God in His grace may choose to shield us from the full fury of the consequences of our sinful choices. He may grant us a pardon from the harsh correction we deserve for a sin that we deliberately choose. Because of His love, He may try to nudge us back on the right track by showing us mercy, not judgment. In fact, He does this all the time.

And yet, we can never presume upon God's grace.

Remember that if you are free, so is God—free to exercise His mercy or not exercise it, according to His desire. He is under no obligation whatsoever to protect you from the unpleasant results of the sin you freely choose. "I will have mercy on whom I will have mercy, and I will have compassion on whom I will have compassion," He proclaims (Exodus 33:19; Romans 9:15).

This means there is a "perhaps" to God's grace.

Yes, He may (and often does, thank God) refuse to "come down" on us when we screw up. The vast majority of the time, perhaps, He shows us His mercy and compassion when we show Him our stubbornness and rebellion. He does this not because He is in any way obligated to do so but because He wants to give us life and joy and peace. He does not want to destroy us. As He says, "As surely as I live, I take no pleasure in the death of the wicked, but rather that they turn from their ways and live" (Ezekiel 33:11). Or as the prophet Jeremiah reminds us, God "does not enjoy hurting people or causing them sorrow" (Lamentations 3:33 NLT).

And yet, there's that "perhaps."

We should *never* take God's grace for granted, as a man named Simon discovered. Simon lived in Samaria, north of Jerusalem, and used to pass himself off as someone great. He boasted in his powers as a sorcerer and encouraged his fellow Samaritans to say of him, "This man is the divine power known as the Great Power" (Acts 8:10). But when Simon saw the *real* power of God as exercised in the ministry of Philip, he felt greatly astonished and quickly thought better of his career. Luke says, "Simon himself believed and was baptized" (v. 13).

To that point, however, the Holy Spirit had not yet been given to the Samaritans, despite their belief. God wanted His Jewish followers who had become Christians to see in a dramatic way that the salvation He offered needed to go to *all* people, not just Jews.

> *God is gracious— but He extends that grace freely, not under compulsion.*

The Jews considered Samaritans half-breeds, part Jewish and part Gentile, the sad result of Assyrian conquests long ago. But when Peter and John visited Samaria, they laid their hands on the new believers and these Samaritans, too, received the Holy Spirit. What a stir it caused! Unfortunately, this gave Simon a bad idea. He approached the apostles and offered to pay them in return for the same power they had shown.

Peter indignantly answered, "May your money perish with you, because you thought you could buy the gift of God with money! You have no part or share in this ministry, because your heart is not right before God. Repent of this wickedness and pray to the Lord. *Perhaps he will forgive you* for having such a thought in your heart. For I see that you are full of bitterness and captive to sin" (Acts 8:20–23).

Was Simon a Christian? It appears so; he "believed and was baptized." The grace of God had swept him into the kingdom. Yet the process of transformation had only just begun. He still thought along old, evil lines. His former habits as a sorcerer still plagued him. So he committed a terrible, public sin—and Peter let him know that his conduct (in this case, a wicked "thought in your heart") had placed him in grave danger. Peter called upon Simon to repent and pray to the Lord. And then—*perhaps*—the Lord might shield him from the consequences of his sin.

Simon understood his great peril. Immediately he begged Peter, "Pray to the Lord for me so that nothing you have said may happen to me" (Acts 8:24).

God *is* gracious—but He extends that grace freely, not under compulsion. There is a "perhaps" to grace. We dare not take it for granted—even though we remain free to do so.

Do What You Will

Centuries ago a great Christian advised his fellow believers to "love God and do what you will." He meant that those who truly love God—those who with their whole hearts seek to do God's will above their own—can live in exquisite freedom, liberated by their Savior from the poisonous impulses of their fallen human nature.

Those who learn to live by this principle can experience the same kind of expansive living. And as they exercise their freedom, more and more they will *want* to freely choose God and what He wants for them.

Steve Brown, host of the *Key Life* radio broadcast, tells a wonderful story about the time Abraham Lincoln visited a slave market.[5] (Steve admits the story might not be true, but it's fun to tell anyway.) At the market Lincoln noted a young, beautiful black woman being auctioned off to the highest bidder. He bid on her and won. He could see the anger in the young woman's eyes, and no doubt knew she was thinking, *Another white man who will buy me, use me, and then discard me.*

As Lincoln walked off with his "property," he turned to the woman and said, "You're free."

"Yeah. What does that mean?" she replied.

"It means that you're free."

"Does that mean I can say whatever I want to say?"

"Yes," replied Lincoln, smiling, "it means you can say whatever you want to say."

"Does it mean," she asked incredulously, "that I can be whatever I want to be?"

"Yes, you can be whatever you want to be."

"Does it mean," the young woman said, hesitantly, "that I can go wherever I want to go?"

"Yes, it means you are free and can go wherever you want to go."

"Then," said the young woman with tears welling up in her eyes, "I think I'll go with you."

In His grace, God has given you the freedom to choose how you want to live. You can go where you want to go, do what you want to do, say what you want to say. I just hope that you remember Who it is that gave you such freedom—and that you'll want to go with Him, wherever He wants to take you.

16

Live Worthy

Most of the time, I loved the purple jacket. Usually I looked forward to wearing it come Friday. Still, every once in awhile—I have to admit—I felt embarrassed by it.

The jacket in question marked its wearer as a member of the Purple Knights basketball team. We had to wear the blazers to school on game day and keep them on when we traveled to and from away games. They immediately identified us as representatives of the Beloit Memorial High School basketball program.

As I said, most of the time I liked putting on the jacket. I enjoyed the idea that it branded me as a member of a select group of student athletes. It felt good to wear the school color and have friends and young ladies come up to me in the hall and say, "Good luck tonight!"

On the other hand, sometimes the jacket felt like a royal pain. For one thing, as a fashion statement, it came up *way* short. Who would wear a used purple blazer to look good? For a second thing, wearing the jacket meant more than that you played for the Knights. The coaches made it clear that if you wore the jacket, you were expected to act in a certain way. If you didn't stay on your best behavior, you might lose the jacket—and all that it represented. A few of my teammates disregarded these warnings, did things to embarrass the program, and found themselves jacketless on game day.

While I never lost the blazer due to unacceptable conduct, my senior year I did find out how it felt to walk around school on game day

155

without wearing purple. Coach Barkin unexpectedly cut all but three seniors, and I found myself playing in the intramural leagues. Only then did I fully realize what a privilege that purple blazer represented. Did it "cost" something to wear the dorky thing? Sure, if you worried too much about stylin'. But I have to tell you, it felt like a much higher cost when I no longer had the right to wear it at all.

Only by Grace

Before we continue about what it means to "live worthy" as a Christian, I need to review what it *doesn't* mean. While I had to earn the right to wear a purple blazer through my efforts on the basketball floor, nobody "earns" the right to play on God's team. None of us can perform well enough to make His squad. If we "make the cut," we do so only by grace.

The young man we know as "the Prodigal Son" understood this as well as anyone. Jesus tells his story in Luke 15. In essence, this young guy from a wealthy family demands and receives his inheritance long before his father dies. Flush with cash, the boy heads to Vegas, picks up women and huge casino tabs, and after months of partying, spends his last dime. Once his money runs out, so do his new "friends," and he winds up on Skid Row. He eventually gets a job cleaning filthy toilets in a rundown rescue mission and has to get used to eating stale bread and diluted vegetable soup. One day as he's mopping up yet another transient's "accident" in the bathroom, a thought occurs to him. *What am I doing here? Back home the servants eat chicken cordon bleu and snack on French pastries. They sleep in warm, clean beds and smell bowls of lavender potpourri, not floors reeking of vomit. I'd be better off working for my dad than staying here and risk catching a terminal case of tuberculosis.*

So he leaves Vegas and begins to hitchhike home, a trip of several weeks. All the way he rehearses what he plans to say to his father. He'll have to eat crow, but he no longer cares. And what he says, he means. "Father," goes his rehearsed speech, "I have sinned against heaven and against you. I am no longer *worthy* to be called your son; make me like one of your hired men" (Luke 15:18–19).

If you know the story, you know that he never gets to deliver his whole speech. Before he can get to the "make me like one of your hired men" line, his overjoyed father interrupts and loudly commands his servants to get the house ready for a huge fiesta. He directs them to burn his son's stinking rags and clothe him instead with the finest Armani wardrobe on the estate.

The happy father in Jesus' story outfitted his son in expensive clothes not because the kid deserved it but because the father loved him. The son didn't earn that love or work for it—in fact, if anything, he had worked *against* it—but the father gave him an expensive blazer to wear (probably not purple) despite what he'd earned. That's grace. The son admitted, "I am no longer worthy to be called your son," and he was right. The father never contradicted his boy's statement. The son knew he hadn't earned his father's favor—and yet the father gave it to him anyway. Why? Because it was the nature of his father to do so. He delighted in grace.

> *He is the kind of God who delights in grace.*

This is how Jesus pictures God's gift of grace to us. Even though we have a great pedigree (made in God's own image), we turned our backs on God to enjoy "a good time." When the fun stops, however, and we find ourselves hungry and on our knees on a grimy, germ-infested bathroom floor, some of us "come to our senses." We call out to God, turn our backs on our worthless choices, and ask Him for mercy. He gives not only mercy, but grace, and noisily welcomes us into His household with great fanfare and the promise of staggering riches. Why? Because we deserve such royal treatment? Hardly. Rather, because He is the kind of God who delights in grace. So in this sense, we never become "worthy" of what we receive.

So what does the Bible mean when it tells us to "live lives worthy of God"? How can genuine grace enable us to live "worthy"? And how can we live in this way and yet avoid the kind of madhouse striving that leads to legalism and a joyless, grim existence?

Worthy of Jesus?

Just as blazer-wearing Purple Knights might behave in a way to bring dishonor and scandal to the school basketball program, so Jesus tells us there is a way that grace-wearing Christians can behave to bring dishonor and scandal to the household of God.

"Anyone who loves his father or mother more than me is not *worthy* of me," Jesus said, and "anyone who loves his son or daughter more than me is not *worthy* of me; and anyone who does not take his cross and follow me is not *worthy* of me" (Matthew 10:37–38).

Jesus does *not* mean that those who do love Him more than mother or father or son or daughter somehow earn their salvation. He does *not* mean that if someone willingly puts his or her life on the line for Him, then that person has succeeded in paying the entrance price to heaven. So what does He mean? He means that He is the greatest prize in God's treasure vaults, completely worthy of our highest allegiance and best efforts—even though that means putting His desires over any contrary wishes expressed by mother or father or son or daughter, or publicly identifying with Him even if it means ridicule, scorn, or worse.

> He is the greatest prize in God's treasure vaults, completely worthy of our highest allegiance and best efforts.

In the last book of the Bible, a resurrected Jesus puts a positive spin on what it means to "live worthy." In chapter 3 He both rebukes and comforts the members of a church who lived in an ancient city named Sardis. Their devotion and commitment to Jesus had largely died, and because of that, Jesus tells them, "Your deeds are far from right in the sight of God" (Revelation 3:2 NLT). Still, even in such a dying church, some believers continued to grow in their faith. Of them Jesus said, "Yet even in Sardis there are some who have not soiled their garments with evil deeds. They will walk with me in white, for they are *worthy*" (3:4 NLT).

Jesus promised that, one day, these men and women would wear a *white* blazer not because they earned it but because they lived in a way that fit their calling as Christians. By faith they acted in a manner that reflected the very nature of God, their Father. And for this Jesus calls them "worthy."

Worthy Saints

Paul and the other apostles picked up on this idea of living worthy of God. Dozens of times the writers of the New Testament use a certain word group to encourage believers to act in a way that matches their status as sons and daughters of the Living God.

The Greek term *axios* and its relatives appear almost fifty times, mostly in the Gospels and in Paul's letters. In thirty-six of those appearances translators have rendered the word as "worthy" or something like it. Time after time the Bible encourages us to live in a way that fits the calling we have received.

This biblical challenge to "live worthy" reminds me of the instructions I got when I put on the purple blazer. I didn't earn the right to wear the jacket by the way I acted in public, but my coaches insisted that as long as it draped my bony shoulders, I had to conduct myself in a way that spoke well of the Purple Knights. The jacket had to "fit," not just physically, but in the way I behaved.

With that in mind, note the many times Paul and others encouraged their believing friends to draw on their faith and so tap into God's grace, thus changing the way they lived.

- "I ask you to receive her in the Lord *in a way worthy of the saints* and to give her any help she may need from you, for she has been a great help to many people, including me" (Romans 16:2).
- "They have told the church about your love. You will do well to send them on their way in a manner *worthy of God*" (3 John 6).
- "As a prisoner for the Lord, then, I urge you to live a life *worthy of the calling* you have received" (Ephesians 4:1).
- "Whatever happens, conduct yourselves in a manner *worthy of the gospel* of Christ" (Philippians 1:27).
- "For you know that we dealt with each of you as a father deals with his own children, encouraging, comforting and urging you to live lives *worthy of God,* who calls you into his kingdom and glory" (1 Thessalonians 2:11–12).

Paul develops this theme more at length in Colossians 1:10–14. In this passage he tells his friends that he has been praying for them "in order that you may live a life *worthy of the Lord.*" Yet here he goes on to explain in more detail what he means by living "worthy of the Lord." To the apostle, living worthy of Jesus means that you and I "please him in every way: bearing fruit in every good work, growing in the knowledge of God, being strengthened with all power according to his glorious might so that you may have great endurance and patience, and joyfully giving thanks to the Father, who has qualified you to share in the inheritance of the saints in the kingdom of light." He also leaves no doubt about where the power to live such a worthy life comes from. He declares that Jesus "has rescued us from the dominion of darkness and brought us into the kingdom of the Son he loves, in whom we have redemption, the forgiveness of sins."

> *The only way you and I can live worthy is to live by faith.*

When you determine that you want to live a life worthy of God, Jesus doesn't ask you to grit your teeth and attempt to do all the "religious" things you really don't want to do. You can't walk worthy by self-effort. Nor can you do so by keeping rules or by trying harder or by digging deeper or by starting a new self-discipline kick. The only way you and I can live worthy is to live by faith. We learn to live worthy by consciously and continually relying on God's grace to do in us what we cannot. This is what Paul means by "the obedience that comes from faith" (Romans 1:5).

God blesses faith-powered obedience because it relies on Him, not on us. Faith honors God by admitting that our own resources come up drastically short, whether we're talking about our ability to save ourselves from hell or our ability to make ourselves into people who increasingly resemble Jesus Christ. When we obey God by grace through faith, He gets the glory and we discover the joy of living in a way worthy of Him.

Worthy Is Worth It

My senior year of high school, I really missed wearing that old, hand-me-down purple jacket. I served as sports editor of the school newspaper and so I still had a connection to the team, but it just wasn't the same. As I recall, my intramural team finished first in the league, but it didn't feel the same, either. I had no idea how much I'd miss the blazer until I could no longer wear it.

Do you sometimes feel embarrassed by the requests Jesus makes of you? When everyone else is wearing the hottest, most daring fashion, do you sometimes cringe at the thought of putting on the spiritual equivalent of a purple jacket? If you ever feel like that, know that you're not alone. I have felt (and sometimes still do feel) the same way.

Still, I can't help but remember my senior year, the one without the purple jacket.

Don't let anyone talk you out of "living worthy." Don't let *yourself* talk you out of it, for that matter. Living worthy is worth it.

So let me ask you a question. Do *you* want to live worthy of God? Does the desire to:

- please God in every way
- bear fruit in every good work
- grow in the knowledge of God
- strengthen yourself in God's power
- develop great endurance and patience
- joyfully give thanks to the Father

beat strongly in your heart? Would you like one day to hear Him say to you, "Well done, good and faithful servant!" (Matthew 25:21, 23)—or something more along the lines of, "Glad you're here, but you'll have to spend a few days bathing in the river of life to get out that awful, smoky stench"?

We don't set our hearts on "living worthy" in order to earn God's love or win His favor. Nor do we exert ourselves to live worthy out of fear that, otherwise, we might lose His love or His favor. No! We live worthy to delight God's heart and to experience our own greatest joy.

And what could be more worth it than that?

Discussion Study Questions

Chapter 1

1. How would you describe "grace"? What is it designed to do?
2. What's wrong with "Christian is as pagan does"?
3. Does God give us His grace to enable us to live for Him or to give us the security to sin in safety? Explain.
4. If you are a believer in Christ, why do you think God saved you?

Chapter 2

1. Is sin more like a pet or a predator? Why?
2. How can "little sins" be just as dangerous as bigger ones?
3. What does sin do by its very nature?
4. In what way is sin "wild"? Fast-acting? Deadly?

Chapter 3

1. Do you think God blushes? Explain.
2. Do you think God "winks" at sin? Explain.
3. In what ways is Jesus more than our "Good Buddy"?
4. Why is salvation not "free fire insurance that allows you to play with matches"?

Chapter 4

1. Why aren't "being nice" and "being gracious" the same thing?
2. In what ways do you think grace can sometimes be "hard"?
3. Can God's grace ever cause someone to feel uncomfortable? Explain.
4. How can you fear God without being afraid of Him?

Chapter 5

1. Why do you think God put certain warnings in the Bible?

2. If you're a believer, who owns your body? Why is that important?

3. Is it possible for someone who loves Christ also to love the thing that murdered Christ? Explain.

4. How can you begin to ask, "what's right with it," more than you ask, "what's wrong with it"?

Chapter 6

1. Why does waiting tend to test our faith?

2. How do you respond when someone mocks your faith?

3. How do we sometimes "hold to a form of godliness" while "denying its power"?

4. Do you love Jesus today more than when you first believed? Explain.

Chapter 7

1. Why is a me-first attitude so destructive to a healthy faith?

2. How do we sometimes set our hearts on "things below"? What's the problem with doing this?

3. Who among your Christian friends do you find it most difficult to get along with? Why?

4. When you pray, do you really expect God to answer? Explain.

Chapter 8

1. What's wrong with "marshmallow grace"? What's the problem with "jawbreaker grace"? How would you describe *real* grace?

2. Why do you think Jesus responded in very different ways to (a) "sinners"; (b) His own disciples; and (c) the leading religious leaders of His day?

3. How do you think God's grace can, right where you are, most effectively move you toward Jesus?

4. Are your desires showing any signs of changing since you placed your faith in Christ? Do you ever find yourself *wanting* to do the things that God asks you to do, when you used to hate them? Explain.

Chapter 9

1. Why do you think God makes such a big deal out of obedience to Him?

2. In what ways does obedience matter?

3. Why is it dangerous to ask, "How far can I go and still be OK?"

4. How does grace enable us to obey God?

Chapter 10

1. When a friend asks you to join some activity that you believe is wrong, do you have a hard time saying no? Explain.

2. How does grace teach us to say no to sin?

3. How do we take off "deeds of darkness" and put on "the armor of light"? What does this process look like?

4. How can pondering the return of Christ help us to live in ways that please God?

Chapter 11

1. Do you like the phrase, "Let go and let God"? Why or why not?

2. What kind of effort are you expending in your partnership with God to become more like Jesus?

3. How would you describe your own "labor" for God?

4. What kinds of rewards are you looking forward to for your faithful, grace-powered labor?

Chapter 12

1. How is grace like a catalyst? What changes does it provoke in us?

2. What kind of "new you" does God want? Describe it.

3. What do you think is God's highest goal for you?

4. What steps are you taking to work with God in transforming you into someone who increasingly acts like Jesus?

Chapter 13

1. How can Jesus live through you by His Holy Spirit? What does that look like?

2. Do you regularly interact with some mature believers? If so, what do you do with them? If not, why not?

3. Why is living by grace more like an adventure than a cruise?

4. Why is it to our advantage to have a Guide rather than a full-featured map?

Chapter 14

1. What does it mean to "die by grace"?

2. What does it mean to be "crucified with Christ"?

3. Why do you have to keep crucifying your evil desires?

4. How can talking to yourself help you to grow as a Christian?

Chapter 15

1. What does "freedom" mean to you as a Christian?

2. How can you best use your freedom? How could you abuse it? What might be the result if you did?

3. What does it mean to "presume" upon God's grace? What's the risk in doing so?

4. What does it mean to "love God and do what you will"? Do you think this is good advice? Why or why not?

Chapter 16

1. How does grace make it possible for you to "make the cut" on God's team?

2. What does it mean to be "worthy" of Jesus?

3. Why can't we "walk worthy" of God through our own efforts? What's the only way to accomplish this worthy kind of walk?

4. Why does God want us to "live worthy" of the gospel? What does this accomplish?

Notes

Chapter 1

1. *The Portable Curmudgeon,* John Winokur, ed. (New York: NAL Books, 1987), 65.

2. A. F. Walls, "Christian," in *New Bible Dictionary, Second Edition* (Wheaton, IL: Tyndale House Publishers, 1982), 186.

Chapter 2

1. *Dumb, Dumber, Dumbest: True News of the World's Least Competent People,* John J. Kohut, ed. (New York: Plume/Penguin Books, 1996).

2. This and following references to the Yacolt snake bite incident are taken from Holley Gilbert, "Man Nearly Loses His Life After Kissing Rattlesnake," *The Oregonian,* B01.

3. www.mountainx.com/weird/2002/1218weird.html.

4. www.Atlanticville.gmnews.com/News/2002/0516/Front_Page/039.html.

Chapter 3

1. Jacques Steinberg, "From Religious Family to Reins of Deadly Cult," *New York Times,* March 29, 1997, as it appears at www.rickross.com/reference/heavensgate/gate10.html.

2. Frank Bruni, "Cult Leader Believed in Space Aliens and Apocalypse," *The New York Times,* March 28, 1997, as it appears at www.rickross.com/reference/heavensgate/gate6.html.

Chapter 4

1. *A Greek-English Lexicon of the New Testament,* 2nd ed., William F. Arndt and F. Wilbur Gingrich, eds. (Chicago: The University of Chicago Press, 1979); *eulabeias,* p. 321; *deous,* p. 175.

2. Leon Morris in *The Expositor's Bible Commentary,* vol. 12, Frank E. Gaebelein, gen. ed. (Grand Rapids: Zondervan, 1981), 145.

3. John Piper, *The Pleasures of God* (Portland, OR: Multnomah Press, 1991), 204.

4. Ibid., 205–206.

Chapter 6

1. Robert L. Thomas in *The Expositor's Bible Commentary,* vol. 11, Frank E. Gaebelein, gen. ed. (Grand Rapids, MI: Zondervan, 1978), 321–22.

2. Frank McCourt, "God in America," *LIFE* magazine, December 1998, 63–64.

Chapter 7
1. Acts 20:28.
2. 1 Corinthians 6:19–20.
3. Philippians 2:3.
4. See Colossians 3:1.
5. John 3:1–2.
6. John 19:38.
7. Mark 15:42–43.
8. See Acts 13:5, 13 cf. 15:2, 36–39.

Chapter 10
1. A. M. Stibbs in *The New Bible Commentary, Revised* (Grand Rapids, MI: Wm. B. Eerdmans Publishing Co., 1970), 1185.
2. Glenn W. Barker in *The Expositor's Bible Commentary,* vol. 12, Frank E. Gaebelein, gen. ed. (Grand Rapids, MI: Zondervan, 1981), 331.

Chapter 11
1. Homer A. Kent in *The Expositor's Bible Commentary,* vol. 11, Frank E. Gaebelein, gen. ed. (Grand Rapids, MI: Zondervan, 1978), 128.
2. See also 1 Samuel 26:23; Proverbs 19:17; Jeremiah 17:10; 31:16; 32:17–19; Matthew 16:26–27; Romans 2:6; 1 Corinthians 2:5–15; 2 Corinthians 5:9–10; Colossians 3:23–24; Hebrews 10:35–36; 11:6, 24–26; Revelation 11:18; 22:12; etc.

Chapter 12
1. Jeff Bollier, "Legendary Beloit coach Barkin dead at 79," *The Beloit Daily News,* December 6, 2002. www.beloitdailynews.com/1202/bern6.html.
2. David Boehler, "Beloit coaching legend passes away," *JS Online, Milwaukee Journal Sentinel,* December 7, 2002, www.jsonline.com/sports/prep/dec02/101403.asp.
3. Bollier, 2.

Chapter 15
1. Don Yaeger, "Bad Behavior: How Mike Price met his Destiny at a strip club," May 12, 2003, *SI Online,* www.sportsillustrated.cnn.com/si_online/news/2003/05/07/mike_price.
2. Mike Lopresti, "COMMENT: No second chance at Alabama for party-minded coach," May 5, 2003, *Tucson Citizen,* www.tucsoncitizen.com/sports/wildcats/5_5_03price.html.
3. "Price dismissed by Alabama," The Associated Press, May 5, 2003, www.msnbc.com/news/908631.asp.
4. Ibid.
5. Steve Brown, *A Scandalous Freedom* (West Monroe, LA: Howard Publishing Co., Inc., 2004), 12–13.